THE WISDOM OF THE ZEN MASTERS

THE AUTHOR

Irmgard Schloegl was born and brought up in Austria where she read for her doctorate in Natural Sciences. Since coming to England in 1950 she has developed her interest in Zen Buddhism and spent twelve years in Japan undergoing traditional Zen training. She is now librarian at the Buddhist Society in London and very much concerned with student training and counselling.

THE WISDOM OF
THE ZEN MASTERS

TRANSLATED
BY IRMGARD SCHLOEGL

A NEW DIRECTIONS BOOK

Manufactured in the United States of America
New Directions books are printed on acid-free paper
First published clothbound and as New Directions Paperbook 415 in 1976
by arrangement with Sheldon Press, London

Published simultaneously in Canada by Penguin Books Canada Limited

Library of Congress Cataloging in Publication Data

Main entry under title:

The Wisdom of the Zen masters.
  (A New Directions Book; 415)
  A companion volume to Thomas Merton's The wisdom of
  the desert and Geoffrey Parrinder's The wisdom
  of the forest.

  1. Zen Buddhism—Quotations, maxims, etc. 2. Zen
  Buddhism—Japan. I. Schloegl, Irmgard.
BQ9267.W57   294.3'927   75-42115

ISBN: 978-0-8112-0610-5

New Directions Books are published for James Laughlin
by New Directions Publishing Corporation,
80 Eighth Avenue, New York 10011

ELEVENTH PRINTING

TABLE OF CONTENTS

FOREWORD BY
CHRISTMAS HUMPHREYS

BEFORE attempting to understand the strange but fascinating sayings of the Zen Masters, of which Dr Schloegl gives here such an admirable selection, it may be helpful to glance at the unique place of the Zen School in the field of Buddhism, a place which seems to have no equal in the whole field of religion.

Gautama the Buddha lived in North-East India in the sixth century B.C. According to tradition his disciples assembled after his death and agreed from collective memory a large body of his sermons. These were in due course committed to writing, and form the Pali Canon which are the scriptures of the Theravāda or Southern school, practised today in Ceylon, Burma, and Thailand. This is the oldest surviving school of Buddhism, and forms at least a magnificent moral philosophy or way of life.

But soon, as is the way of all religions, there were schisms, partly on points of doctrine, partly on substantial developments of various aspects of it. This development moved in different and sometimes opposite directions, yet all the schools so formed in the next thousand years stem alike from the Buddha's Enlightenment, and the basic principles seem to be common to all.

The most profound development was built about the name of Nagarjuna (second century A.D.), one of the greatest minds in Buddhism. His Madhyamika school, a 'middle Way' between the extremes of nihilism and eternalism, ruthlessly destroys belief in any separate thing, and proves that everything in Samsara, the world we live in, is empty, void, and collectively No-thingness. All things exist in the ordinary sense of the term but no thing exists separately.

This doctrine, set out in the famous literature of 'the Wisdom that has gone Beyond', is the metaphysical background to the school of Zen, but is far beyond mere philosophic argument. It is based on the spiritual experience of men who thought to the end of thought and then went far beyond it. Here is the mental platform from which the Zen devotee, encouraged by his Master's training, leaps into the unknown and finds—the Self within. And when he finds himself he finds that he is all other selves, all equally one with the same Buddha-mind, and that indeed 'there are no others'. As we read in *The Voice of the Silence*: 'Look within, thou *art* Buddha.'

Yet even this great height of consciousness must be expressed in, and therefore limited by, thoughts or concepts and the scriptures formed of them. But the Buddha's Enlightenment was in very essence a breakout of this realm of concept, with its fetters of duality. Gautama finally became the Buddha when he merged in the Beyond of concept, in the No-thingness which is at the same time Allness, the living Whole of what he called 'the Unborn, Unoriginated, Unformed', which has a thousand names but no existence which our minds can comprehend.

The time came when this ultimate concept and its implications in the spiritual development of man were taken from India to China. According to tradition it was in the sixth century A.D. that Bodhidharma, a famous Indian sage, arrived in the capital and being a distinguished scholar was invited to the Emperor's Court. The interview which followed is surely one of the most dramatic in the history of religion.

The Emperor asked his visitor: 'Since the beginning of my reign I have built so many temples, copied so many sacred books and supported so many monks. What do you think my merit might be?'

'No merit whatever, Sire,' replied the sage.

'Why?' demanded the Emperor astonished.

'All these are inferior deeds,' replied Bodhidharma, 'which would cause their author to be born in the heaven worlds or on this earth again. They still show traces of worldliness. . . . A true meritorious deed is full of pure wisdom, and its real nature is beyond the grasp of human intelligence. . . .'

The Emperor then asked his visitor, 'What is the first principle of the holy Doctrine?'

'Vast emptiness', was the reply, 'and nothing holy in it!'

'Who, then, is now confronting me?'

'I know not, Sire,' said Bodhidharma.

This strange and violent attitude was the very antithesis of the Indian Buddhists of the day, but the Chinese loved it. Why write a volume to describe what may be impressed on the mind in a word, or by a gesture, or even a blow with a fly-whisk?

A pupil once arrived at his Master's house exhausted from playing polo. 'Are you tired?' asked the Master. 'Yes, Master.' 'Were the ponies tired?' 'Yes, Master.' 'Was the goal-post tired?' . . . It was not until the middle of the night that the pupil suddenly 'got it', and wakened the Master to tell him so. The Master was pleased. This was far more effective for the Chinese mind than a volume of sermons to prove that Life is one and indivisible!

Bodhidharma's basic theses of the transmission of truth without reliance on words or scriptures, and the need for 'direct pointing to the soul or Self ("heart-mind") of man' made sense to the Chinese, though it makes no sense to the logic-ridden Western mind. Whatever be the merits of other schools of Buddhism, each with its scriptures and formulated doctrine, the Zen Masters of China and Japan returned full cycle to the Source of Buddhism, the Enlightenment, and henceforth concerned themselves wholly and fully with the Enlightenment already existing in every mind though clouded still with illusion.

The implications in Nagarjuna's teaching are unique in religious history. If in every mind burns a flame of the Buddha's Enlightenment there is nothing to seek and nothing to acquire. We *are* enlightened, and all the words in the world will not give us what we already have. The man of Zen, therefore, is concerned with one thing only, to become aware of what he already is, of the Self within, of his inseverable Oneness with the total Buddha-Mind.

Meanwhile this mind is wedded to thought/feeling,

and each is sadly clouded with desire for self, the most virulent illusion of all. These thoughts and desires all work in the field of duality in concepts themselves pressed into the mould of words. As such they can never contain, much less express, Truth, and not even the noblest intellect can ever *know*. It can study the opposites each in turn but can never with thought alone attain the state before division, when the opposites are seen still undivided, as totally, and at the same time, both. Thus truth and falsehood are seen by the enlightened mind as dual aspects of the Truth; the ugly and beautiful as dual modes of Beauty; good and evil as both subsumed in Good. And these are truly known as a triple aspect of That which alone forever *is*, the Fullness/Void, the Absolute.

How can this 'pre-bifurcation' state, as Dr Suzuki calls it, be achieved? How can the Self in illusion be once more merged in the Self which is? The answer is by developing the faculty by which alone each human mind will 'see', in the Zen sense of true seeing, things as they really are. This is spiritual awareness, when the seeing is one with the object of sight. Each Master has his own methods of rousing the intuition, of 'awakening' the mind to abide nowhere, to be free from the shackles of concept and its false duality.

But on the pure foundations of sound morality, with motives largely purified of self, the pupil will in time and with enormous effort suddenly see that 'there is nothing infinite apart from finite things', and that indeed, as the Master Hui-neng said, 'All distinctions are falsely imagined. Here is the first taste of that 'timeless moment' of satori, the experience of non-duality. This is the opening of the true path of Zen.

Dr Irmgard Schloegl will soon need no introduction to students of Zen Buddhism. With a sound knowledge of Chinese and Japanese written records, and some twelve years' training under two Rinzai Zen Masters in Kyoto, she has a distinguished career before her. By translation, original writing, and personal teaching in the Zen tradition, she is helping to make known the true purpose of the Zen school of Buddhism. This new volume, small in size but large indeed in worth, will help to establish her growing status, and is a valuable addition to the small library of genuine works on Zen by Western writers. I am grateful for the opportunity to help present it to the Western Buddhist world.

The Buddhist Society
London

PREFACE

I HAVE been asked to compile a short book on 'The Wisdom of the Zen Masters', comparable to Father Merton's *The Wisdom of the Desert*. I accepted this task with a mixture of hesitation and joy. The former because I know too well how inadequate I am and the latter because it gives me an opportunity to express in my limited way my deep gratitude to the long line of the Zen Masters and my two teachers. Dead or alive, their vitality, directness, and solidity have greatly impressed me in the course of some twelve years of training as a lay student attached to a traditional Rinzai Zen training monastery in Japan.

The chosen selections, though they follow a general pattern, are entirely subjective. They include Chinese and Japanese Masters both past and present, read or heard. Where English translations were available, I have made use of them. My thanks are due as follows:

A First Zen Reader, *comp. and tr. Trevor Leggett. Tuttle 1972, for all quotations from Master Sessan.*

The Ox and His Herdsman, *tr. Tsujimura-Trevor. Hokuseido Press, for all quotations from Master Otsu.*

Zen and Zen Classics, *Vols. I, II, III, tr. R. G. Blyth. Hokuseido Press, for short quotations from various Masters.*

Zen: *Poems, Prayers, Sermons, Anecdotes, Interviews, ed. and tr. L. Stryk and T. Ikemoto, Doubleday Anchor Original, for the story of the poor Samurai.*

The Cat's Yawn. *First Zen Institute of America, New York, for the quotation from Master Sokei-an on Zen as a religion of tranquillity.*

I wish to thank Mr Trevor Leggett and Mr Christmas Humphreys for reading the manuscript, and for their many helpful suggestions.

Last but not least my thanks are due to Mr Christmas Humphreys who kindly agreed to write the Foreword. In the course of some twenty-five years he has been a second father to me, without whom I would never have thought of going to Japan for Zen training. My gratitude is great indeed.

THE WISDOM OF THE ZEN MASTERS

*

STORIES AND SAYINGS

THE WISDOM OF THE
ZEN MASTERS

WHAT is Zen and who are the Zen Masters?
What is the ground that nurtured them in a
cultural environment different from ours?

Zen has become fashionable, and we are apt to talk
about it as if it were a Thing: something is 'Zen' or
'zennish'. This only shows that our Western mind has
been fascinated by a word or term and now uses it
within its own frame of reference. There is no such
thing as 'Zen'; if anything, it is a process.

The word 'Zen' is derived from the Sanskrit
Dhyana, which in Chinese transliteration became
Ch'an, and in the Japanese pronunciation 'Zen'. It
means meditation, contemplation, pondering. So it
stands for the meditation school of Buddhism. Like all
definitions, this is misleading, for meditation is not the
only nor even the main training device used.

As a Buddhist School, Zen is firmly based on the
fundamental Buddhist teachings common to all such
schools. These are the Three Signs of Being: impermanence, non-I, and suffering. We carry an unneces-
sary load of suffering because we cannot accept
impermanence and non-I. We cannot accept them
because of the Three Fires that burn in us: wanting,
hating, and delusion. The Four Noble Truths, based on
these premises, are: there is suffering, physical and
mental dis-ease; there is a cause for this suffering (see
above); this cause can be worked out, can be brought

3

to an end, for whatever has a beginning is bound to have an end; there is a way out or deliverance from this suffering, by means of treading the Noble Eightfold Path.

The first step of the Noble Eightfold Path is usually translated as 'right views'. This translation is perhaps unfortunate because it carries the connotation of opinion or notion, and it is 'I' that has views and opinions, which does not correspond with the Buddhist premise of non-I. A look at the Chinese rendering of this term is useful for in Chinese it may be read as 'right seeing' or, idiomatically translated into English, 'clear seeing'. To try to see clearly is, then, the first step along the Noble Eightfold Path, which as a way of training is indeed calculated to dissolve the blinkers of emotion-fired egoism, and leads to that clear seeing which is the beginning and the end of training.

Driven by the Three Fires—our main emotional roots—'I' whirls on the Wheel of Life, Samsara, with its Six States, from moment to moment and from life to life. Or it imagines itself to do so, to be bound upon that Wheel. If clear seeing ensues and in that clear seeing no 'I' is to be found, the Fires are extinguished and there is deliverance from the Wheel, or from the 'ocean of birth and death' as the Zen texts are fond of putting it.

However, we have to be careful when we read such statements. For it is just the 'I' that would like to be eternal. in other words secure, that has been seen through and dissolved. What an I-less state is we cannot conceive; even a state of a somewhat diminished

4

'I' is difficult to grasp unless some training has been undergone to that end. Nor is it helpful to ponder what it is that is reborn if basically there is no I.

A further and eminently practical point is that as long as I feel strongly 'I', it is no good denying this 'I'. Calling it an abstract proposition does not diminish it in me, it merely makes me a hypocrite. And since 'I' is nourished by the Three Fires, by our passions or emotions, it is not the cutting off of emotions, for that is impossible, but the valid transformation of the emotional household that extinguishes the Three Fires and so weans the 'I' from their influence.

We have thus approached the basis of Eastern religions, which take divinity as immanent in creation. Buddhism, being a non-theist religion, does not call this immanence a divinity, but refers to it as the Buddha Nature, the Heart Ground, or just the Heart. This Heart is, of course, not to be taken as the 'red lump of flesh', the physical organ in our physical bodies, but in the sense of the 'heart of the matter'.

To become aware of the Heart, clear seeing is needed. But it is not a state to be attained, made, or fashioned for we have our being in it anyway. It is rather a sloughing off or wearing away of the obstacles in us which are preventing us from being aware of the Heart.

These are basic Buddhist principles. What then distinguishes the Zen school? It is a school of Northern Buddhism or Mahayana, which developed what are perhaps the deepest philosophical and psychological systems ever known. But inherent in them is also the danger that one can easily become stuck at the intellectual or word level. It seems that the Zen school is a reaction against just that, a kind of unspoken return to the basic principles of Buddhism. It insists on personal experience and insight. Being aware of the glibness of words, it stresses the showing of insight-understanding, the clear seeing and actual expression of it.

The question 'What is "cold"?' can be answered intellectually in terms of degrees centigrade. We set the freezing point at zero centigrade, and scientifically postulate an absolute freezing point as well; a subjective graduation can be made from cool to chilly to cold. All this can be rationally explained by a man who has never left the Equator. The Zen way of expressing it might well be an involuntary shiver at the mention of 'cold'—which presupposes that the state of being cold has actually been experienced.

Since this kind of expression, too, lends itself to empty imitation, the Zen school traditionally insists on trained and proved teachers who can help their students to walk the way they have gone themselves, and who can confirm their clear seeing, their insight-understanding. This assistance is called transmission. The Zen Masters are guides rather than teachers.

The Buddha, a man like us, walked the way of awakening. It is his footsteps that guide us. As the heir of a little kingdom at the foot of the Himalayas, he is said to have been brought up in a very sheltered environment, but educated as was fit for his standing. The learning of his time was at his disposal, and we are told that he excelled in it.

When in the four fateful outings from his father's palace he encountered a pauper, a sick man, an old man, and a corpse, we must not assume that he had never heard of such things, only that for the first time in his life he had come face to face with them; hence the impact that became a burning problem and changed the course of his life.

We know that he left the palace and in the tradition of his time became an ascetic, that he trained under the two best teachers available, and that each considered him worthy to become his successor. He declined both times because his own problem was still unresolved. So he left them but continued a life of great austerities on his own which attracted some disciples. However, his problem remained while his austerities brought him close to death. Deciding that this course could not bring him to the solution, he took some food and had a bath, whereupon his disciples left him as an unworthy ascetic. It was only now, forsaken by everything, that he sat down alone under the Bodhi Tree, resolved not to get up before he had found his way through, to sit it out once and for all, come what may. And one morning he did 'see clearly' and became the Awakened, the Buddha.

An unspoken question worth pondering is: would he or could he have done so without his training under his two teachers?

We need a guide as even the Buddha did, or we are bound to go astray. We need to imbibe the available learning of our time, whatever that time may be. Thus we become fully 'man'. Lusting after the fruits of the Bodhi Tree while shirking the process of becoming man is truly childish and regrettable. For it is said that of the Six States on the Wheel of Life (page 4) deliverance can be won in the human state only, the state of man. Deliverance and Awakening are synonymous terms: they imply awareness of being awake, a condition different from the unconscious unity of the infant that is still in the state of innocence. That state we have lost in the process of growing up, and had to lose so as to become man and as man find our way to it in awareness. 'Only when one has reared a child can one know a father's kindness', as a Zen Master put it.

But for genuine Awakening more is needed than becoming man and acquiring an acquaintance with cultural values and background. In that quest man is alone as was the Buddha when he sat down under the Bodhi Tree. He needs to be shorn of everything, as was the Buddha—no longer a prince; seasoned in a life of poverty; no longer the outstanding disciple and heir-elect of a famous teacher; left by his own disciples as too lax in his austerities.

It seems a grim prospect, but it does bring man to rock-bottom where in stark nakedness all thought-coverings, all protecting screens are gone. In their absence the seeing becomes clear of itself.

What the Buddha added to the wisdom of his time, and what we sorely need today, is the insight that here are no mechanical techniques on the inner way, and that no extreme means, by themselves, will produce clear seeing. He himself had carried his austerities to the utmost and found no answer in them: his problem had remained. Hence he preached the Middle Way—not only as neither too much indulgence nor too much ascesis, but in a deeper, more existential sense, as he himself declared: 'Suffering I teach, and the Way out of Suffering.' This we have to consider carefully. The Middle Way, even in this wording, does not imply rejection of suffering, but a way through suffering, as it were a thoroughfare, to the end of it.

Bodhidharma said of this Way: 'Be prepared to sweat white beads, for it means to endure what is unendurable, and to bear what is unbearable.' This is its nature, and it does sound frightening and forbidding. After we have come through it, the skeleton of fear that sits on the neck of each of us topples down. 'I' has been reduced and 'softened' in the process, and since only 'I' can know fear, non-I equals no fear. 'I' is for ever separate, hence insecure, alone, frightened. 'I' excludes not-I, all that is 'other', and so rejects the greater part of life and of what is.

But if there is no more fear there can be no more rejection. If nothing is rejected then, as Master Rinzai puts it, 'what at the moment is lacking?' And if nothing is lacking, there is 'nothing further to seek', another of Master Rinzai's maxims which he considers the most precious. For if nothing is excluded, nothing rejected, it means totality, wholeness, fulfilment, completion—not a rigid inactivity but 'lively as a fish playfully leaping'. It is true deliverance from the bonds of 'I', and the immanent heart with all its warmth and joy then functions freely, for the obstacles have been removed. It has been uncovered, re-discovered, become aware of—but not attained.

The Zen Masters are not only masters of that lore, they are masters of that Way. Which means that they are masters of themselves. They sum up this process in their short and succinct manner which shuns big words: one has to climb to the top of a hundred-foot pole, and from the top of it 'take a step further', says one; another, 'jump down'. It comes to the same thing. They understand each other well.

When reading Zen texts, it is useful to keep in mind a distinction which is generally maintained. The 'Buddha' stands for the immanence which is indescribable. The historical man who became what we call the Buddha is referred to as 'Shaka', the abbreviation of 'Shakyamuni', teacher of the Shakya clan or tribe.

The Zen school[1] developed in China, where in contact with the concrete and practical Chinese mind it sloughed off its Indian dress and within a few generations became thoroughly Chinese. The Indian path or Marga, the way to be trodden *to* a goal, became under Taoist influence the Tao, the Way which *is* its own goal and which is inherent in everything that is. Indeed the very term Tao is shared by both Buddhists and Taoists.

In this process of naturalization Confucian ethics came in as it were by the back door. They seem to have been instrumental in ending the mendicant life dear to

[1] There are two excellent books on the historical development of the Zen school:

H. Dumoulin, *History of Zen Buddhism*. Faber.

H. Dumoulin and R. F. Sasaki, *The Development of Chinese Zen*. First Zen Institute of America.

Indian Buddhism. Monks now began to settle down in endowed communities. It was from these communities that the early Zen Masters broke away, preferring life in some remote mountain area. As a result the community growing round them had to be mainly self-supporting. Manual labour became one of the training devices, and still is.

Master Hayakujo, who laid down the rules for such a community and whose rules are still basic in Zen monasteries, stated the position simply as, 'a day without work is a day without food'. There is the story that when he was getting rather old and feeble his monks begged him to cease from working, to no avail. Fearing for his health, they finally resorted to hiding his working tools. Whereupon Master Hayakujo refused to eat, following his own precept just quoted. The monks returned his tools.

What, then, is the Tao, the Way that is its own goal? A 'true man of the Way' is another way of describing the 'man who has nothing further to seek', the 'independent man of the Way' who leans on nothing and who has the 'single eye' or has come to see clearly.

The classic Taoist text is the *Tao Te Ching*, 'The Way and its Virtue', also translated as 'The Way and its Power'. It is a short text, and perhaps no other of comparative length has been translated so often and so variously.

Tao, the Way, has the connotation of a physical path actually to be walked. As theory only, it would not affect a practical mentality. But it is not a processing machine from which, neatly packed, identical products emerge. Bodhidharma, traditionally the founder of the Zen school, is supposed to have said: 'All know the Way; few actually walk it.'

So the Way exists for the one who actually walks it as best he can, and keeps walking whether the going is smooth or rough. By this exercise the walker gets the use of his legs and develops strength of muscle as well as endurance. His eyes get used to recognizing stumbling blocks, slippery ground, pitfalls, quagmires, and other obstacles. When his strength and sure-footedness are well developed, the Way ends—in nowhere. From now on he can be trusted to make his own way. Well used to the Way and to himself, he is sure to find one, making it as he goes along.

The second term in the title *Tao Te Ching* refers to the strength that develops from walking the Way. If translated as 'virtue' it is in the sense of 'by virtue of'. Hence it does not connote a moral value but it is that depth from which morals and moral strength arise.

Tao and *Te* are complementary. In man, *Te* is the function of *Tao*. Both are intimately related and inseparable.

By virtue of walking the Way, the childish 'I want', the passions or emotions, are transformed. What in fact happens is that the energy (strength) loses the blind compulsion of a drive and becomes amenable to conscious choice. In this lies the virtue of seeing clearly and of being able to act in accordance with that seeing. This embraces all the truly human qualities, such as responsibility, justice, consideration, warmth of heart, joy, tolerance, compassion, aware-

12

ness of strength of personality and its power and limits. For nobody has the right to manipulate anybody or to impress anybody with his stronger personality, not even for the other's imagined good, for nobody can know what that good is. This is courtesy rather than callousness, for the other's dignity is thus acknowledged, or the dignity of his grief is respected. If and when he is ready, the other will of himself reach out for consolation and feel free to ask for a hand to point out the way.

This is the place where the man of *Tao* and *Te* stands, and his way is 'action by non-action', refraining from all meddling in or interfering with things small or great. He is acting rightly because he acts with the whole of himself just when action is called for, instead of throwing himself like a spanner into the wheel of things, blindly, for the sake of doing something. A meddler has no rest and is prone to bring destruction in his wake. With whatever good will, to shout and awaken a sleep-walker on top of the roof will not help. It is better to wait quietly till he comes down and awakes. Then a gentle suggestion is in place so that precautions can be taken, the arrangements being left to him. The other is not a baby; he has his dignity and needs it sorely.

Such is the virtue of the man of Tao, by virtue of which he is free and this is his strength. Obviously this is not brute strength of muscle or mind which always imposes. Brute force is the reverse of the strength of restraint, of doing nothing when nothing is required.

While the walker follows the Way, the Way itself

is the discipline which produces clear seeing and the strength to act in accordance with it. Then the Way ends; the walker is free of the Way, free of his own I-biased and deluded seeing. He himself has become the Way. So he acts out of his own nature.

We are now better equipped to consider the traditional teaching and training of the Zen school, and where the Zen Masters point.

Traditionally, the Zen school claims its origin from the Buddha himself. When he was to preach to a large assembly at Rajagriha he looked round and, without uttering one word, just raised a flower. Of the huge audience none understood but his main disciple Kasyapa, who smiled. The Buddha said: 'I have the priceless jewel of the Dharma Eye, and I now hand it to you, Kasyapa.' This incident started the 'transmission from heart to heart'.

The Indian monk Bodhidharma is said to have brought this school to China. His future successor Eka after long perseverance finally gained an interview with him. Zen Masters have never been propagators. Eka's plea was that since his heart was not at peace, Bodhidharma should set it at rest for him. The latter retorted: 'Bring me your heart and I will set it at rest.' Eka, after consideration, admitted that however he searched for his heart he could not find it. 'There,' stated Bodhidharma, 'I have set your heart at rest.'

Bodhidharma summed up his teaching as:

A special transmission outside the teachings;
Not standing on written words or letters.

Direct pointing to the human heart,
Seeing into its nature and becoming Buddha.

When the succession after the Fifth Patriarch was under consideration, his main disciple Jinshu was generally expected to be the heir. To present his insight, he composed a verse:

> The body is the Tree of Awakening,
> The heart is a bright mirror;
> Carefully wipe it always
> So that no dust can settle.

Eno (Hui Neng), who in fact became the Sixth Patriarch, countered with another verse:

> There is no Tree of Awakening;
> The bright mirror has no stand;
> When all is emptiness
> Where can dust settle?

The teaching analogies of the Zen school are finely balanced, and these two verses reflect each other like two mirrors. They make a point that is as important now as it was then: one cannot have the one without the other; the chicken comes out of the egg; without the egg, no chicken.

Many of the Zen Masters are claimed as fathers or founders of special teaching lines, stressing a particular way or style. Their teachings and biographies were written down by their disciples. They themselves wrote nothing; they taught. What they taught was not scriptural learning, not Buddhism or Zen, but a way of life. Familiarity with the scriptures is basic to all

Buddist monks. The Zen Masters made use of the scriptures and quoted them freely, though often with a comment that brought new light on what had become too familiar. They tried to break down blind piety towards the teachings, and to help their students to a real insight, to that clear seeing as a result of which the scriptures assumed a new and living meaning —not something abstract 'up there' to be quoted, but functioning here and now in one's own life and in all that is, 'clearly perceptible right before the eyes'.

The Zen Masters were men of few words, but mature in insight and skilled in means. They were also past masters in rousing their students out of complacency and in spotting imitative behaviour. They could be fierce to an extent that to us seems appalling, though never without purpose, but balanced by a 'grandmotherly kindness' which seems to have been a greater danger than their fierceness, for we often find warnings in the texts against spoon-feeding.

A man who wants to stand squarely on his own feet and to get his sight clear needs courage to see into his emotional household and to disentangle himself to some extent from it. Such a man in the fullness of time needs to come to a genuine breaking point at which 'I', fired by passion, abdicates. This is what Master Hakuin called the Great Death, and that this is a shattering experience is obvious.

To help to bring about this turning over, to assist what is in itself a natural process as a kind of midwife, is another of the functions of a Zen Master. The Zen analogy for it is a hen hatching out an egg. When the chicken is ready, the hen must peck the shell to help the chick out. If this is done too early or too late, the chick dies. Hence derives the very real responsibility assumed by a Zen Master, of which he is humbly conscious. The relationship is a serious contract, binding on both parties.

Every inner experience has a convincing, even overpowering finality. The little ones in particular are inevitably followed by 'I have got it', an I-appropriation. 'I' wants to hold it, which is impossible. Then 'I' strives to get it back, which is equally impossible for 'I' has no say in the matter. The wanting and striving to bring it back is misdirected effort, is clinging to a passing phenomenon, and so only strengthens the sense of 'I'. This is contrary to the Way, and so the Way is lost.

Hence one more function of a Zen Master is to prevent students from becoming stuck in any experience and thus losing the Way. He goads them on in their training till sooner or later they die the Great Death, and come to that true humility which is the joy of the heart, releasing its inherent warmth which now can flow and act freely. When the trammels of egoism are gone, its blinkers shed, what remains and is seen is what is.

A monk brought two potted plants to his Master. 'Drop it,' ordered the Master. The monk dropped one pot. 'Drop it,' again ordered the Master. The monk let the second pot go. 'Drop it,' now roared the Master. The monk stammered: 'But I have nothing more to drop.' 'Then take it away,' nodded the Master.

The simplicity of such an analogy must not blind us to the veritable impossibility of doing just this. And yet it has to be done. Hence the importance of training.

Even dropping what we have, all we have, is not an easy thing. But dropping what has us, our ingrained opinions, views, ideals, our dear burdens that we so hotly and volubly defend—we cannot drop them by an act of will. It is just that which is the rub. We never even dare to look at them squarely, much less to doubt their validity.

The Zen Masters hold that three things are necessary for this training: a great root of faith, great doubt, and great courage-endurance. The death of 'I' is no easy matter. Moreover, it needs preparation so that the dying can happen cleanly.

A knight in medieval Japan deserted his liege lord after long inner struggles, for such an action was inconceivable according to the code of knighthood. He did it because he felt an overwhelming vocation for the Zen life. Having spent some twelve years in one of the mountain monasteries, he set out on pilgrimage. Before long he encountered a knight on horseback who recognized him and made to strike him down but then decided against it as he was unwilling to sully his sword. So he just spat in the monk's face as he rode by. In the act of wiping away the spittle, the monk realized in a flash what in former days his reaction would have been to such an insult. Deeply moved, he turned round towards the mountain area where he had done his training, bowed, and composed a poem:

The mountain is the mountain
And the Way is the same as of old.
Verily what has changed
Is my own heart.

Such is the Way of Zen. Who could exhaust it? The guides on that Way are the Zen Masters. It is a Way that can be walked now as then. The guides are there still. They do not propagate either themselves or their teachings. They sit and train themselves, and those who come to them prepared for such training, able to bow at least the head and capable of giving up cherished views. 'The Great Way is not difficult, it only avoids cherishing opinions' on questions such as what is Truth, the Absolute, or other great words.

A Zen Master was asked whether Zen should not be propagated to some extent in our times which are in such need of its qualities. Would not more availability, some publicity, public sermons and the like be useful? His answer was both characteristic and a fundamental summing-up. He replied that, after carefully pondering the question, he could not see any positive harm resulting from such propagation. As to the good it could do, he was extremely doubtful. For even if it did not just go in by one ear and out by the other, even if it produced a sizeable uplift, by the time the person had gone home and sat down to the family dinner, it would all be gone. The real propagation, he thought, would be for the would-be propagators to settle themselves down and cleanse their own hearts yet again. For in so doing there springs up in the human heart such a deep fountain of love that it cannot possibly be contained in one's own heart, but needs must flow. And since everybody, even the worst criminal, has that same human heart which is directly touched by such love, words are really not necessary. There is a coming into the ambience, a touch, a link, and the person so touched may of his own volition start walking the Way.

This Way is not something unknown. The Buddha himself never claimed that he had found something new, only that he had rediscovered an old Way leading to an ancient city. Nor did he want to initiate something new. 'Suffering I teach, and the Way out of Suffering.'

We from another cultural background, with another mentality, tend to try to fit this into our mechanical world-model of pressing buttons and swallowing pills for a desired and preconceived result. This is why we are so keen on and concerned with end-states. We never consider that there are no 'states' through which we 'progress'. It is simply that by training our own attitude changes. But we cannot conceive how that may be; we can only think about it from the point where we are, which is bound to be different, or 'totally other'.

We live in a dual world of night and day, of darkness and light, of joy and sorrow. We are part of this world. Both aspects are there. If we want light and joy only and reject the other half, we shall begin to feel that a vital part of life is missing. But since only a masochist enjoys suffering, it is a razor-edge line on which to hold the balance.

Perhaps it is possible for each of us when we go into ourselves to see that there is a dividing line between the bitter resentment of selfishness, the 'why must it happen to me?', and the grief and sorrow that is part and parcel of our human condition. The latter needs to be accepted and lived; all life needs to be lived. We live it in any case; but how we live it is important. If we reject what is common to all, go through it with averted eyes, and refuse our share of common sorrow though we all expect if not demand our share of common joy, then the unlived, refused life piles up against us as fear, including the fear of death.

Master Shaku Soen liked to take an evening stroll through a nearby village. One day he heard loud lamentations from a house and, on entering quietly, realized that the householder had died and the family and neighbours were crying. He sat down and cried with them. An old man noticed him and remarked, rather shaken on seeing the famous master crying with them: 'I would have thought that you at least were beyond such things.' 'But it is this which puts me beyond it,' replied the master with a sob.

Have we ever bothered to think out the consequences of a hypothetical state free from suffering? What we want, badly, is not to be bothered or hurt any more; but this would make us also incapable of feeling warmth and joy. We should turn into unfeeling monsters, callous and selfish brutes. Should this be the way of Buddhism which holds to the twin pillars of wisdom and love?

Love, warmth of heart, in its accepting humility is

a true blessing. And it is the way that Buddhism cultivates. It is a way out of suffering not through refusal but through total embrace. This is what we need to know if we want to understand the Zen Masters, or if we happen to feel inclined to walk that way ourselves.

It is also a way to a true understanding of oneself. A true understanding of oneself, without excluding anything, is at the same time an understanding of others. And being so hard to achieve, it gives rise of itself to tolerance and compassion, to that disinterested love which is open, free, and, like the sun, just there. 'I' with its ever-present itch to interfere, however altruistically 'as I think it ought to be', has abdicated. With the irritant gone, the itch ceases. The intentional 'do-gooder' is proverbial because all react against him though his intentions are undoubtedly good.

We have tried to better the world, and ourselves, for millennia, and though we have seemingly succeeded in some things, in others we are worse off than ever. Every short-term improvement inevitably throws up its opposite which trips us up.

Is there a way out? Yes, the hardest, for it starts at our end, where it hurts. The way is for each of us to dismantle our own obstacles. We all want to be reasonably considerate, reasonably tolerant, reasonably warm-hearted; why can we not be so, or not always so, though we ourselves want to be? What prevents us against our will? Truly, we are our own obstacles. And since the world is populated by us, we make and shape our own weal and woe. Could a fair number of us dislodge no more than our own obstacles, we need not trouble ourselves about the world, for it would of itself be a better place to live in. Could it be that 'I' finds it more congenial to try to change the world than to set to work on its own obstacles and so change itself? Yet, our world would thus be a better one.

This way the Zen Masters show by living the lives they did and do. They actively contribute to it by their own lives and by training their students to live such lives. They are conspicuous for the absence of any zeal to interfere or to better anything. All of them shun abstractions and speculations, however edifying and lofty, as 'flowers in the empty sky'—at best useless, more often downright destructive. Their common motto through the ages is 'look at the place where your own feet stand'. A Chinese proverb often quoted by the Zen Masters says: 'Even a journey of a thousand miles starts from right under one's feet.'

If one's eyes are searching for imaginary flowers in the sky, if one's head is in the clouds, one is apt to stumble and to lose one's way.

A present-day Master said of his students, in their presence, that they seemed to like him, and that occasionally they would set out to do something 'great' for him that would really please him. He could see it coming on in the far-away look in their eyes which were glued to the 'great things'. He did not damp their enthusiasm outright as they had to learn the consequences; but he resigned himself to a period of trouble. Their minds away on the great, they would forget the ordinary things such as opening or shutting the temple gates, and they burnt the rice, spoilt the vegetables, and so on. After some days when all were beginning to feel the strain and to suffer from indigestion, he would tell them that if they really wanted to please him, would they please abandon the 'great thing' they were going to do for him, and just do the ordinary things they had to do as well as they could; nothing would please him better.

That is typical of the way in which Zen Masters 'teach'. They are not teachers in the usual sense of the word, but they are eminently practical. Compact and solid, they stand on their own feet and they know human nature. They point the Way for their students, so that they do not lose themselves in the 'thorns and brambles' of speculation, or in the regions 'where fierce desire rages, and opinions stand up like spears on a battlefield.'

Though many of them, both in China and Japan, have enjoyed imperial patronage, and some of them have counted emperors as their disciples, they have preferred the monastic life and fare within their community. Nor would they leave their community for long; the responsibility is binding.

The sun shines; that is its nature. Clouds may obscure it to our eyes; they do not affect the sun. These obscuring clouds we need to dispel so as to become aware of the sun. Such clouds we fashion by our I-interests, intentions, volitions, passions. Indeed we are our own obstacles.

The Buddha Nature is in us, as in everything that exists. If we do not obstruct it with our desires, etc., be they good or bad, it acts of itself, through us. This, however, is the opposite of 'as I want it, everything goes'. The very 'I' that wants everything 'my way' is the cloud that is to be dispelled.

In the training, so much depends on one's own effort that there is an ever present danger of 'I' getting a swollen head. Hence it is said that three qualities are necessary for the training: Great Faith, Great Doubt, and Great Effort. Great Doubt is rather like chewing food very finely to render it digestible and prevent stomach trouble. Great Faith, or at least 'the root of Great Faith', is indispensable, as it is the quality of bowing the head at least in respect for something perceived as greater than 'I'. 'I' is a stiff-necked fellow; bowing the head is an age-old gesture of laying down 'I'. There is much bowing in the Zen training. Great effort explains itself.

In the training, one must strive to give up everything—and the stress here is on the 'inner acquisitions', such as notions and views and convictions rather than on goods and chattels; to apply oneself singlemindedly, with total effort and concentration; and to die the Great Death. As one of the Zen problems puts it: 'A man hangs on by one hand to a root over a sheer precipice. Can he open his grip and let go?' What Zen training can do is to hang a man on that precipice; but there is the root that brought him there in the first place, and to that he will cling with tenacious desperation. Only he himself can relinquish that grip when he is ripe. And so it can be said that the Zen training produces the ripeness for letting go of the precipice as well as the hanging on it; but the man himself must let go.

At one stage or other most of us have been forced on such a precipice by life itself. What distinguishes the man of Zen is that he then actually lets go. From the precipice he falls on to his own two feet. Standing on them, he has nothing more to seek. Nor does he lean on anything. He no longer trespasses and crops on another's field.

The general Buddhist analogy is the ocean and the waves. Blown up by the storms of passion, waves rage, racing and toppling each other. Each wave is individual; each wave is but ocean. As wave it rises and sinks; inherently it remains what it ever has been—ocean. To see this with clear eyes, to accept one's ocean nature, or Buddha Nature, and to live from it, solves also the problem of fear and death. And, indeed, most other problems are then solved. Death, too, is a fulfilment, if only we can see it thus. Were the Zen Masters so vitally alive because they had no fear of death? And did they stress the clear eyes because of it? 'Coming or going, always at home.' 'In the trackless the path comes to an end.'

Does a wave leave a trace in the ocean? The Zen Masters, 'mingling their eye-brows' in union over the centuries, 'leave no trace'. Their wisdom is indeed perennial. Yet they are ordinary men. As they themselves stress, 'the nose is vertical, the mouth is horizontal'.

Their doing and the unhindered life which flows in it cannot be pressed into any framework. This freely playing life, the 'Samadhi of Play', is truly beyond laws and rules—but it is also from this source that all moral values and religious rules arise. Beyond laws, it is not lawless! It is the inexhaustible source of creativity, of all art, and of a quiet and profound humanity. Such men have themselves become the Way. How could they go against it?

To allow this freely playing life always to be present, some qualities are necessary, and they have to be developed along the way. 'I' is subject to 'highs' and 'lows'. Not so the heart. Only 'I' wants/hates/fears, etc., something, for 'I' is exclusive of 'other'. Just this constitutes the insecurity of 'I'.

The Three Fires (page 3) are the link between 'I' and object. Without such a link the object as such is neutral and, subjectively, it leaves me cold. Hence, what makes me feel hot with regard to the object is my reaction to it of desiring or rejecting or fearing or whatever, irrespective of whether this 'object' is concrete or abstract, a mouse or an ideal. The fire is in me; it is my delusion which makes me think it is 'outside', in the object.

So, I want something. If I think of the various things I have wanted hotly—including my opinions, ideals, notions and the like—I see that the objects of my wantings are shape-shifters, for no sooner have I got what I so much wanted than it palls on me. Only as long as I want it does the object seem to have an irresistible fascination, a real power over me. I feel that once it is 'mine', I shall live happily ever after. But after I have got what I so hotly wanted, it loses its attraction, and after a period of restlessness another 'enticing' object catches my fancy—equally hotly pursued. Whether it be a new hat, a new car, a new house, or a new idea or notion, has little to do with it. Again, in themselves objects are neutral; what touches me is my reaction to them.

Watching this swing of our wants is a useful exercise. The smaller wants are easiest to observe: they change often; they are easily fulfilled; and their fascination is not too overwhelming—so they are good training material. If we do this watching within a gentle discipline, we may find that the objects of our wants change so much that it is not so much the objects that I want, but rather that I want what suits me, I want my will, or what I fancy.

So, having set out with 'I want something', I am now left with a truncated 'I want', which casts around until it snatches at a suitable object, concrete or abstract. Now I know what I want. The old delusion has once again taken hold of me.

Paradoxically, what I *really* want I do not know, I cannot know it, for a picture has arisen which veils it. 'I' is the picture maker. It is possible by the practice of a discipline to gentle and tame 'I', and so to wean 'I' from the fashioning of pictures. Then what is left from our sentence of 'I want something' after both the picture (something) and the picture maker (I) have dropped off, is what I saw as want, what no 'I' can see as it is, and what has been called the Heart, the Buddha Nature. Words here do not matter; they are only terms, pointers at best and as we now know, there

is the ever-lurking danger of picture making! 'I'
can never know it; 'I' is its own obstacle. The trouble
is the picture-making propensity of 'I'—a malfunction.
Without the picture-making itch, there is just
reflective consciousness, of which intelligent thinking
is one function among others.

What did the Buddha say when he awakened?
What struck him more than anything else, the first
words that he uttered? 'I have seen you builder of the
house—the ridgepole is broken—never will you build
new houses again.'

This house builder, the picture maker, cannot be
seen. In itself it is not. What gave rise to it can be seen
into, genuinely and concretely, but only in a state
when one is 'naked and alone', shorn of all attributes and
attainments, as the Buddha was when he sat down under
the Bodhi Tree (page 7), when truly there is no-thing.

The Zen Masters are guides to help their students to
this insight. Master Eno (Hui Neng, the Sixth Patriarch)
demanded: 'Show your true face which you had before
your father and mother were born.' Surely that is not
an 'object' whether concrete or abstract; least of all
is it 'mine'. Master Joshu, when asked by a monk
whether a dog has the Buddha Nature, pointed
directly in his reply, 'No-thing'. And Master Hakuin
joins them with his terrifying question, 'What is the
sound of one hand?'

Over a thousand years in time separate Master Eno
and Master Hakuin; but in their insight they 'knit
eyebrows' together. It tallies. How could it not? In
the Heart Ground there is no such thing as 'modern' or

'ancient', or east or west—indeed, there is no-thing.

There is no-thing—always and everywhere. What a paradox! We are living beings in our dual world of night and day, of dark and light, of joy and sorrow. We are truly of it in that we are part of it. In us, too, is the seeming paradox of being.

From the dark night of no-thing the sun rises and we see the 'ten thousand things'. Such a sight is likely to bewilder us, especially with the dazzling light of the sun in our eyes. In the dark of night we see nothing, and so everything is the same, of one darkness. But in the light of day a tree is a tree, and a house is a house. If we do not wish to be tossed about by circumstances, we have to learn to see the differences clearly; and without the picture maker there is no judgement involved, only differences clearly seen. I am I and you are you, and we are not the same in the light though we come from the same lineage. 'In the landscape of spring there is nothing better nor worse; the flowering branches grow naturally long or short.' And so there is respect and understanding for the other, acceptance of my own limitations, and consideration for our human lot.

Climbing mountains, an inexperienced person may sometimes be overcome by giddiness or fear. This usually happens at an exposed place, where there is real danger. Neither going forward nor going backward is apparently possible. If it seems a real impasse, the guide may have to resort to a slap in the face. The emotional reaction to this resolves the impasse and makes movement again possible.

Zen Masters also use this means to bring about a

change in a stalemate situation. If Zen stories are read out of context, as a collection of 'highlights' as it were, without knowledge of the actual training process, it may seem that a lot of slapping and hitting goes on. A mountain guide does not slap his trainee haphazardly; and the Zen Masters are guides skilled in means. The training requires that the disciple, too, acquires skill in means, skill in using situation and circumstances, skill in making do with what is at hand.

The Buddha taught The Middle Way. There is little to choose between leaning so far back as to lose one's footing and falling flat on one's face. To incline to the left or to the right is equally dangerous. Master Rinzai stresses 'the independent man of the Way who leans on nothing', for the essential thing is to lean on no-thing, and thus to keep to the Middle Way. When we have come to see things rightly we live a full life, a real life.

There is a legend that the infant Buddha, when born, took one step in each direction and said: 'In heaven and on earth, I alone am the World-Honoured One.'

We know that Prince Gautama became the Buddha, the Awakened One; that like us he was a man who was born and died. How could a new-born babe walk and talk? Moreover, taken on the word level, his statement sounds aggressively arrogant—had it been uttered by a man. But in the mouth of an innocent baby, how direct the legend is, how correctly it points! 'That' the peasant uses every day without knowing it, as an old Zen saying has it. And the 'awakened' knows it—that is all.

But with this realization one of the fundamental

human problems is seen into—death. And as a result most other problems are also dissolved. In the old Buddhist analogy of the ocean and the waves, if a 'wave' awakens to its ocean nature, is it likely to be unduly upset by its rising and sinking back? Though the points of emergence and re-merging are indeed momentous ones, the wave is ever contained in the ocean, is of the ocean, can never be separate from it; its essential ground and being is the ocean in all its vastness and strength.

This is what the legend of the infant Buddha proclaims, loud and clear. What the Awakened, the Buddha, taught was suffering, being caught in 'wave only', and the way out of this suffering, opening the eye of wisdom, realizing the ocean nature. It is not a question of something to be gained, but a genuine and valid change of attitude. For this, training is essential. The mind has many notions, it is a notorious windbag. Only a true change of heart is of itself productive of sufficient energy for training practice. Old habits die hard. Hence the many analogies of forging, hammering, or refining. The wave-'I' needs to be pruned, cut back, before the ocean-nature can become clear. A wave not blinded by itself, were it conscious, would know of the way up and the way down; every rise and fall bring back new experience—and so the rise and fall are meaningful.

What is important is how we live our lives. And the wonderful thing is that, once this is realized, then our life has of itself taken on meaning and purpose, it has become 'full', when it seemed empty before. And death, too, is a fulfilment. If there is no fear of it, the 'way down' is as clear as the 'way up'.

The Zen Masters knew their return. It was, and is, their custom to say farewell to their disciples, and often they used to write a so-called 'death-poem'. Is this so strange in the clear light? 'The peasant uses it every day without knowing it.'

We fear death because we are caught in the 'wave only'. And because of this we do not really live fully spending ourselves. Thus unlived life piles up against us. Moreover, we no longer see people die. Truly death has become an unclean word with us; the dignity and majesty of Death are lost.

There is no room for sentimentality in Zen training; one might call it a luxury that cannot be indulged in. Adulation and flattery are equally out. But the master-disciple relationship is a binding one. It is also a relationship of utter sincerity, of a stark nakedness in which there is no room for play-acting or mummery. It is as dangerous as a naked sword or goading a tiger. In this light, the little repartees take on a different meaning from that which they have when read lightly in a comfortable armchair.

There is no specific 'body of teaching' in Zen. The Zen Masters lead their students in a lively way, by direct example, and by pointing their finger—and warning the students at the same time 'not to mistake the pointing finger for the moon'. The Buddha Dharma, the Good Law of Buddhism, the essence of Buddhism and of Zen, what is it?

Master Rinzai said:

'All deliberation of heart misses the target. All movement of thought goes to a contrary end. If people can understand this, they are not separate from the one here before the eyes. And yet you go burdened with your begging bowl and bag, running about looking for the Buddha and the Dharma. Do you know him who thus runs about seeking? He is lively as a fish in water, and has neither root nor trunk. Though you embrace him you cannot possess him; though you move away from him, you cannot get rid of him. The more you seek him, the farther away he is, and if you do not seek him he is right before your eyes.'

Master Eno said: 'We use it every day without knowing it.' Not knowing it, we are driven around by circumstance. Master Hakuin calls this, 'in the midst of water crying pitifully from thirst'. And Master Rinzai admonishes: 'Cease from running; look, there is nothing lacking.'

There is nothing, therefore, that needs to be 'gained' or 'achieved'. And the difference is not in the 'using', for use it we do anyway, but in our doing so with open eyes, knowingly. This is why when the eyes really open as from a dream, it seems as intimately familiar as 'meeting one's own father at the cross-roads and recognizing him beyond a doubt'. Or as an old Master put it: 'How wondrous, how miraculous, I carry wood and fetch water.' Master Hakuin says: 'Not knowing how near it is, we seek it far away.' We chase the unknown, the wonders, not knowing that we are in the midst of them would we but open our eyes. 'Though gold dust is precious, in the eyes it clouds vision.'

Of the Six Paths of Existence (page 4) it is said that deliverance is possible only from the human state. Though born with a human body, we are not yet really human; we carry in us all states. The work of training is to transform or transmute them, to humanize them. To undertake such a transformation requires mighty effort and is at the same time a true labour of love. (Sublimation is a change of the 'picture' at best; it does not touch the energy flow that gives rise to it. But it is the latter that is in need of transformation or of 'humanization'.) Only when the gods and the demons, the 'highs' and the 'lows', are worked through and out, is a true human being born.

When we meet statements like Master Rinzai's: 'If you meet the Buddha, kill the Buddha', we must not be misled by the seeming surface, especially if the Buddha means little to us. The man who became the Buddha is dead. What he was, 'awakened', cannot be 'found', for it is no-thing. Hence 'awakening' is awakening to an absence of things, such as opinions, notions, ingrained views, and dearest ideals, especially those without which life seems not worth living and on which we have built our very lives—as the sincere believer has built his on Buddha. These are what Master Rinzai, correctly interpreted, tells us we must kill. Only thus can we come into that absence, that spiritual poverty in which opens the 'single eye' which is the heart, opens to what is both one and two, light and warmth.

To take a handful of water out of a living river, and sprinkle the drops about—Master Rinzai warns, 'do not let yourselves be deceived'.

STORIES AND SAYINGS

★ I ★

IN THE Chinese capital of Ch'ang-an there lived an eminent Confucian scholar. He was a gentleman of nearly eighty, and was said to have no equal in his profound learning and understanding of the teachings of Master Kung. Then a persistent rumour arose that deep down in the barbarian south a new doctrine had sprung up that was even deeper than his. The old gentleman found this intolerable and decided that the issue had to be settled one way or the other. And since there was nobody of his own depth of understanding whom he could send, he decided in spite of his age to set out himself. After months of hardship on the road, he arrived at his destination, introduced himself, told the purpose of his visit, and suggested that they should each set forth their teaching and understanding. Then, as two gentlemen, they could decide between themselves whose was the more profound system. His host, who was a Master of the new Zen school, agreed and motioned his visitor to start. It took the old gentleman quite a while to outline his teaching and to elucidate his points. His host listened without one word of interruption. At last the visitor came to an end and asked his host now to proceed with his teachings. But the Zen Master merely quoted: 'To avoid doing evil, to do as much good as possible, this is the teaching of all the Buddhas.' On hearing this, the Confucian gentleman flared up: 'I have come here in spite of the dangers and hazards of such a long and rough journey and in spite of my advanced age. I have honourably told you of my purpose. As agreed, I have shown you the profound teachings, and have held nothing back. And you just quote a little jingle that every three-year-old child knows by heart! Are you mocking me?' But the Zen Master replied: 'I am not mocking you. Please consider that though it is true that every three-year-old knows this verse, yet even a man of eighty fails to live up to it!'

★ II ★

IN a monastery in medieval Japan was an elder monk of whom the young novices stood in much awe—not because he was severe with them but because nothing ever seemed to ruffle or upset him. So they found him uncanny and were frightened of him. Eventually they felt they could not bear it any longer, and decided to put him to the test. One dark winter morning when it was the elder's office to carry votive tea to the Founder's Hall, the novices ganged up and hid in a corner of the long and winding corridor leading to it. Just as the elder passed, they rushed out yelling like a horde of fiends. Without faltering one step, the elder walked on quietly, carefully carrying the tea. At the next bend of the corridor stood, as he knew, a little table. He made for it in the dark, laid the tea bowl down on it, covered it so that no dust could fall into it, but then supported himself against the wall and cried out with shock: 'Oh-oh-oh!' A Zen Master telling this story commented on it: 'So you see, there is nothing wrong with the emotions. Only, one must not let them carry one away, or interfere with what one is doing.'

★ III ★

TWO MONKS on pilgrimage came to the ford of a river. There they saw a girl dressed in all her finery and obviously not knowing what to do, for the river was high and she did not want her clothes spoilt. Without more ado, one of the monks took her on his back, carried her across, and put her down on dry ground. Then the monks continued on their way. But the other monk started complaining: 'Surely it is not right to touch a woman; it is against the commandments to have close contact with women; how can you go against the rules for monks!' and so on in a steady stream. The monk who had carried the girl walked along silently, but finally he remarked: 'I set her down by the river. But you are still carrying her.'

★ IV ★

A YOUNG monk had been under a famous Master for but two years when the old Master died. When the successor was installed, all monks who wished to continue under him went to ask his permission. When it was young Kyogen's turn, the new Master who knew him well asked: 'So here you are, brilliant, with outstanding capacities, knowing all the scriptures by heart! Are you sure you want and need to continue this rough and simple training?' The young man, rather pleased that his capacities were known, indicated that he considered it a good thing to stay for a few more years. The new Master took him up: 'Well, so you are pleased with yourself! You can quote the scriptures by heart—tell me, then, where do you go after you have died?' Kyogen was speechless. His immense scriptural knowledge raced through his mind, but he could not remember any relevant passage. Piqued in his pride and convinced that the answer must be in the scriptures, he asked permission to withdraw so as to look it up. But however he searched, he could not find it. The question gripped him, he was determined to find out, feeling that everything was at stake. So he pored over the scriptures, forgot food and sleep, and within three days was worked up to such a state of tension that he could no longer bear it. Gaining an interview with the Master, he admitted that he could not find the answer in the scriptures, and could the Master please tell him. The Master replied that it was for him to find out, for if he were told, it would rob him of his own insight. Kyogen in the urgency of his problem was beyond reasoning, and now demanded an answer. On the master's stern refusal, he gripped him and threatened to kill him. 'And do you think my dead body will give you the answer?' laughed the Master. At that the tension in Kyogen broke; he realized what he had done. He apologized and left the monastery, convinced that he had lost all his chances in this life. He decided to spend his days humbly and harmlessly as a wandering monk, hoping that in his next life he would thus have better circumstances in which to continue his training. After years of wandering all over the country, he came to the tomb of the Sixth Patriarch which he found derelict and uncared for. He settled down there, restoring the place, keeping the grounds, and looking after the occasional pilgrim. Thus he lived for years. One day, he was sweeping and weeding the grounds as usual, and as he tipped out his barrowful of weeds and pebbles in the back yard, one pebble hit a bamboo trunk with a resounding clink. On hearing that sound he suddenly 'awoke'—and with the awakening the answer to his old question was also clear to him. He cleaned himself up, dressed in his full monk's robes, climbed the mountain behind the pagoda, and there prostrated himself in the direction of his monastery, thanking the Master that even under threat to his life he had not divulged an answer and so robbed him of his own insight.

★ V ★

AN OLD and pious woman had built a hermitage for a monk, and for years brought him his daily food and generally looked after him. One day she decided to test him. She told her pretty niece to bring his meal to him, embrace him, and then at once come back and tell her his reaction.

On being embraced, the monk roughly pushed the girl away, saying: 'Sap rises no longer in a withered tree.' The girl returned and told what had happened. The old woman stormed up to the hut. 'For years I have kept a block of wood!' drove out the monk and burned the hermitage.

★ VI ★

A YOUNG man wished to acquire supernatural powers. After a long search for a teacher he found a Mountain Immortal who consented to teach him on condition that he never asked about or interfered with whatever he might see. The eager young man agreed. He saw a dog beaten badly, and then a man—but he firmly kept his mouth shut and looked the other way. Finally his instructor took him down to hell with him. There he saw both his father and mother dragged forward in chains, and fiends beating them. At that he sprang forward: 'No! stop!' And found himself back in his home village, content, and no longer lusting after supernatural powers.

★ VII ★

AN ELDER monk on his pilgrimage one evening put up in a temple where he talked with another monk also on pilgrimage. The two found that they had much in common, and decided next morning to continue together. When they came to a river, the ferry boat had just left. The elder sat down to await its return. His new friend continued, walking over the water. Halfway across he turned back and motioned the other to follow, calling back: 'You can do it, too. Just have confidence and step on.' But the elder shook his head and remained. 'If you are frightened, I'll help you across. You see I can do it.' Again the elder shook his head. The other walked across, and there waited until the ferry had brought the elder over. 'Why did you lag behind like that?' he asked. 'And what have you gained by hurrying like that?', replied the elder. 'Had I known what you were like, I would not have taken up company with you.' And wishing him good-bye, the elder continued alone.

★ VIII ★

MASTER RINZAI in a sermon to his monks quotes from the scriptures that the Buddha has supernatural powers, and explains what they are. What we usually call supernatural powers are not the Buddha's. After all the demon king on losing a battle made his whole host of fiends, 84,000 of them, vanish in the hollow stalk of a lotus. Would that make the demon king a Buddha? The Buddha's supernatural powers are the true ones, and only a Buddha possesses them: seeing without being deceived by colour and form, hearing without being deceived by sound, smelling without being deceived by smells, tasting without being deceived by tastes, touching without being deceived by touch, and thinking without being deceived by mental configurations.

★ IX ★

MASTER HAKUIN said: 'If a man wants to know the taste of sea water, even if he lives right in the mountains, he has only to set off and go straight ahead; if he keeps going, after some days [the country is Japan] he is sure to come to the sea. Dipping his finger into it and licking off the drops, at that moment he knows for himself the taste of all the seven oceans.'

X

When a boy, Master Hakuin heard a fierce sermon on the tortures of hell, and that same evening when he heard the flames crackling under the iron bath tub (the traditional Japanese way of heating the water), the sermon and the sound merged into one of those impacts that change the course of a life. He became a monk to dissolve his fear of burning.

With that as a spur, he trained assiduously and went through all the ups and downs such training entails. He was twenty-four when he had what to him seemed a tremendous experience—so much so that he thought nobody over the last two hundred years or so had reached such a depth. He wanted to have it attested in the traditional way, but no Master would do so. Young Hakuin was the more convinced, and decided finally to seek out a Master who lived in the Japanese Alps and was renowned for his severity as well as for his understanding. On his arrival there, he presented a poem he had composed to show his insight. The Shoju Rojin accepted it with one hand, stretched out his other hand, and remarked: 'I have received your poem. Now show me your insight!' Hakuin was nonplussed, started to talk, was refused, became determined to show his understanding, and on being refused again and again, stayed on as he felt sure he could convince the Master. The Master on his side treated him with unprecedented severity, calling him 'a devil's child imprisoned in a dark cave', and continually beating him. These clashes between the impassioned young man and the Master steering an exceptional disciple through the final impasse of drunken pride went on for a year. Then one day Hakuin, while begging in a village, became so distrait that he failed to hear the old woman on whose doorstep he stood telling him to go away. She became enraged on seeing what she took to be an impertinent monk still demanding alms after she had told him to leave. Finally losing her temper altogether, she got hold of a broom and hit him as hard as she could. Hakuin fell senseless to the ground, and on recovering 'awakened'. On his return he encountered his Master who gave one look and asked what had happened. Hakuin recounted the events. His Master affectionately stroked him with his fan, and never more called him a 'devil's child imprisoned in a dark cave.' That happened when Hakuin was about twenty-five. Soon after he left his Master and looked after his old temple teacher who had fallen ill. After the teacher had died, he had to take care of his old mother. Then he wandered about for a while and finally settled down in a poor temple. In his own account, he says that he was forty-two when one night he was reading the *Lotus Sutra*. Snow was falling outside. On looking up from his reading, suddenly everything seemed to fall together and to jell. He had had many experiences— now he 'saw'. Tears came into his eyes, and all he could find to say was, 'The Zen training is not easy'. Later on he admitted that, compared with this, his big experiences and the many little ones 'that make one laugh and dance' seemed unimportant.

XI

MASTER SESSO warned: 'There is little to choose between a man lying in the ditch dead-drunk on rice liquor, and a man drunk on Satori.' And of this latter, he said it was like little children at a fair each buying a plastic bag full of water with a goldfish in it. On the way home they start vying with each other, 'Mine is the biggest,' 'But mine is the best colour,' 'No, no, see, mine is the liveliest one', and soon they quarrel in earnest. Then the first stone flies, a bag is ripped, the glittering thing expires, and there is sorrow and lamentation.

* XII *

MASTER SESSO said: 'Though descriptions can be given, what really matters cannot be rendered in words. In front of a Shinto shrine a believer may be seen to pull the straw rope that summons the divinity, then clap his hands three times to indicate he has come to worship, and then with folded hands bow deeply in the Presence. All this can be described down to the last detail. The divinity cannot be seen anyway. But what happens in the heart of the sincere believer in the act of bowing that is the blessing. And that is indescribable.'

* XIII *

MASTER RINZAI said: 'If you know that fundamentally there is nothing to seek, you have settled your affairs. But because you have little faith, you run about agitatedly, seeking your head which you think you have lost. You cannot stop yourself.'

★ XIV ★

WEALTHY donors invited Master Ikkyu to a banquet. The Master arrived there dressed in beggar's robes. His host, not recognizing him in this garb, hustled him away: 'We cannot have you here at the doorstep. We are expecting the famous Master Ikkyu any moment.' The Master went home, there changed into his ceremonial robe of purple brocade, and again presented himself at his host's doorstep. He was received with due respect, and ushered into the banquet room. There, he put his stiff robe on the cushion, saying, 'I expect you invited the robe since you showed me away a little while ago,' and left.

★ XV ★

MASTER RINZAI taught: 'If students come to seek, I go out to look at them. They do not see me. So I put on all kinds of robes. The students at once start speculating about them, taken in by my words. It is all very sad. Blind shaven heads, men who have no eyes, they lay hold of the robes I am wearing—green, yellow, red, or white. When I take those off and put on the robe of purity, the students cast one glance and are beside themselves with joy. And when I take it off, they are disappointed and shocked, run about frantically, and wail that I go naked.

So I say to them: "Do you in any way know me who puts on all these robes?" And suddenly they turn their heads and recognize me.'

⋆ XVI ⋆

MASTER RINZAI warned his students: 'All I am talking about is only medicine appropriate for curing specific ailments. In my talks there is nothing absolutely real.'

⋆ XVII ⋆

MASTER MUMON said: 'The treasures of the house do not come in by the front door.'

⋆ XVIII ⋆

A MONK asked Master Joshu for the Way. 'Why, just there behind the hedge,' the Master pointed. 'But, Master, I mean the Great Way,' persisted the monk. 'Oh, that leads to the Capital,' replied the Master.

⋆ XIX ⋆

TWO MONKS, seeing a flag fluttering in the wind, started discussing it. One said: 'It is the flag that moves.' The other held: 'No, it is the wind that moves the flag.' The argument went to and fro. Master Eno stepped up to them: 'It is neither the flag nor the wind, but the hearts of the two brothers that are flapping.'

⋆ XX ⋆

TWO MONKS were arguing the abstract question of the link between the heart and objective circumstance. Hearing their argument, Master Hogen interrupted: 'This huge stone here, do you say it is inside your heart or outside?' One monk smartly came out with: 'Since everything is in the heart, this stone is too.' 'Your heart must be very heavy,' rejoined the Master.

＊ XXI ＊

OF MASTER IKKYU it is told that he was drinking thick green tea while a tremendous thunderstorm was raging outside. He was just finishing his last sip when lightning struck and hopped about in front of him. Master Ikkyu slapped the tea bowl over it smartly and thus imprisoned it. Lightning began to feel sorry for itself and begged to be let out. The Master, pressing the tea bowl down firmly, refused. On being entreated again, on grounds of compassion, the Master agreed to set lightning free on condition it would never again strike the temple complex. Lightning promised —and indeed to this day has kept the promise (now four hundred years).

＊ XXII ＊

MASTER TAKUAN was asked by a monk whether he ever recited the Amida Buddha invocation. 'No,' replied the Master. 'Why not?' 'Because I fear I might sully my mouth.'

＊ XXIII ＊

ON HIS death-bed a Master was asked by his disciple and Dharma heir: 'Master, is there anything else that I need to know?' 'No,' said the Master, 'I am quite satisfied by and large. But there is one thing about you that still worries me.' 'What is it?' asked the heir. 'Please tell me so that I can set it right.' 'Well,' said the Master, 'the trouble is you still stink of Zen.'

XXIV

A MONK was saying farewell to Master Joshu, who asked him: 'Where are you going?' The monk said: 'All over the place, to learn Buddhism.' Master Joshu, holding up his fly-whisk, said: 'Do not stay where the Buddha is! And pass quickly through a place where there is no Buddha! Do not make a mistake and bring up Buddhism to anyone for three thousand miles.'

* XXV *

MASTER DOGEN advised: 'Do not aim at achieving Buddhahood.'

* XXVI *

MASTER ENGO said: 'If you see horns behind a hedge, you know there are cattle. If you see smoke, you know it comes from fire.'

* XXVII *

MASTER RINZAI said to his students: 'The independent Man of the Way leans on nothing. Do not give yourselves airs, just be your ordinary selves.'

* XXVIII *

MASTER UMMON taught: 'We all have a light inside; but trying to look at it makes it turn black.'

* XXIX *

A ZEN proverb says: 'In the landscape of spring there is nothing better nor worse. The flowering branches grow naturally long or short.'

⋆ XXX ⋆

MASTER SOKEI-AN, who lived half of his life in the United States, stated humorously: 'If you are in a powerful car in the middle of the Gobi Desert, you can step on the gas pedal and go any speed you like, any direction you fancy. But if you are in New York at a busy Broadway crossing, you better look out for the traffic lights.'

⋆ XXXI ⋆

EVERY DAY Master Zuigan held the following conversation with himself: 'Master!' 'Yes.' 'Wake up, wake up!' 'Yes!' 'From now on, do not let yourself be deceived.' 'Yes, yes.'

⋆ XXXII ⋆

MASTER HAKUIN said that the Great Death was the condition for genuine insight. But to keep it, one must die the Great Death several times.

⋆ XXXIII ⋆

AN OLD man always used to come to Master Hyakujo's sermons, and afterwards leave at once. One day he remained and told the Master that long before he had been Master there. A monk had asked him whether an awakened man was still subject to the law of cause and effect, and he had answered that such a man was free from it. Whereupon he had become a fox for five hundred lives. Could Master Hyakujo release him by 'turning the question'? The Master agreed, and the old man at once asked: 'Is an awakened man still subject to the law of cause and effect?' 'He does not obscure it,' stated Master Hyakujo. On hearing this, the old man awakened, bowed his thanks, and as a special favour asked for the cremation of his fox's body according to the funeral rites for monks.

★ XXXIV ★

A MASTER gardener, famous for his skill in climbing and pruning the highest trees, examined his disciple by letting him climb a very high tree. Many people had come to watch. The master gardener stood quietly, carefully following every move but not interfering with one word. Having pruned the top, the disciple climbed down and was only about ten feet from the ground when the master suddenly yelled: 'Take care, take care!' When the disciple was safely down an old man asked the master gardener: 'You did not let out one word when he was aloft in the most dangerous place. Why did you caution him when he was nearly down? Even if he had slipped then, he could not have greatly hurt himself.' 'But isn't it obvious?' replied the master gardener. 'Right up at the top he is conscious of the danger, and of himself takes care. But near the end when one begins to feel safe, this is when accidents occur.'

★ XXXV ★

MASTER MUMON ironically comments on himself: 'He has made it all so clear, it takes a long time to catch the point. If you realize it is foolish to look for fire with fire, the meal won't take so long to cook.'

★ XXXVI ★

An old Master said: 'Turn your heart round and enter the origin. Do not search for what has sprung out of it! When you have gained the origin, what has sprung out of it will come to you of itself. If you want to know the origin, then penetrate your own original heart. This heart is the source of all beings in the world and outside the world. When the heart stirs, various things arise. But when the heart itself becomes completely empty the various things also become empty. If your heart is driven round neither by good nor bad, then all things are just as they are.'

★ XXXVII ★

The Third Patriarch says: 'Do not be attached to either the one or the other. Do not search for them. If one clings to right and wrong even to the least extent, his heart gets lost in the tangle. Both exist only through the one, but do not cling even to the one. If no attached thinking arises, then there is no error in things.'

★ XXXVIII ★

Master Otsu comments on this emptying of the heart: 'The heart becomes empty, the situation quiet, and the body just as it is. When someone succeeds in reaching this point, the mirror of his heart shines clearly and his nature opens wide and clear. He leaves error and does not attach himself to truth. He dwells neither in error nor awakening. He is neither worldly nor saintly. All worldly desires fall away and at the same time the meaning of saintliness is emptied without residue. Such detachment from everything is what Master Rinzai called "the complete taking away of both, of man and situation". Here is experienced absolute not-ness, since self and object allow themselves to come to Nothing. Genuine Zen experience consists exclusively in this "taking away of man and object". This complete not-ness is the original place from which all thinking and knowing spring, but, even if one is permitted to speak of a "place" at all, such terminology is only provisional. Even if one wanted to characterize it as unborn-ness, or as Nirvana, or as truth, one could never hit it. It lies beyond all terminology and expression; thinking cannot reach that far.'

⋆ XXXIX ⋆

MASTER TOKUSAN said on this: 'If you can say it you will get thirty blows, and if you cannot say it you will also get thirty blows!'

⋆ XL ⋆

MASTER GANTO said to a brother: 'Whatever the great masters of Zen say, however they expound the Scriptures, of what use is all their learning and understanding to another person? That which gushes out from your own heart—that is what embraces heaven and earth!'

⋆ XLI ⋆

MASTER MUMON advised: 'Rather than putting the body to rest, rest the heart.'

MASTER RINZAI was fond of asking: 'What, at this moment, is lacking?'

HE ALSO suggested: 'If you meet a swordsman on the road, show him your sword. Do not offer your poem to a man who is not a poet.'

MASTER BASO taught: 'The Heart is Buddha.' Later he changed this particular medicine and taught: 'Not heart, not Buddha.' Master Daibai (Great Plum) had awakened on Master Baso's 'The Heart is Buddha'. To test him, Master Baso sent a monk to question him. Master Daibai told the story of how he had asked Master Baso, 'What is Buddha?' and had awakened on his 'The Heart is Buddha'. The monk said: Master Baso has changed his teaching. Nowadays he says "Not heart, not Buddha".' 'That old fellow, setting out to confuse people! He may say what he likes, I stick to "The Heart is Buddha".' Master Baso, when he heard of this, nodded in agreement: 'The Great Plum is ripe.'

MASTER NANYO, another disciple of Master Baso, instructed his monks. ' "The Heart is Buddha"—this is the medicine for sick people. "No Heart, no Buddha"—this is to cure people who are sick because of the medicine.'

★ XLVI ★

THERE IS a Zen saying: 'The further one breaks into the region of the origin, the deeper the region becomes.'

★ XLVII ★

MASTER OTSU commented on it: 'To reach real gentleness means to let the original nature persist in all circumstances of everyday life.'

★ XLVIII ★

MASTER SESSAN said: 'The secret of seeing things as they are is to take off our coloured spectacles. That being-as-it-is, with nothing extraordinary about it, nothing wonderful, is the great wonder. The ability to see things normally is no small thing; to be really normal is unusual. In that normality begins to bubble up inspiration.'

★ XLIX ★

MASTER SESSAN said: 'There are people who do a little practice and before attaining any spiritual light jump up without thinking at all and come out with pointless big words and fine phrases. They go in for every kind of oddity to show how different they are and think carelessness and unreliability are spiritual freedom. Wit they pass off as enlightenment and frivolity as detachment; they specialize in speaking and acting as if mad.'

MASTER OBAKU, who was often seen bowing with great devotion, was asked by a disciple: 'Are you seeking something of the Buddha, or seeking something concerned with the Truth?' The Master replied: 'I have nothing to ask of the Buddha or to seek about the Truth.' 'Then why do you worship?' The Master said: 'I simply worship.'

MASTER SESSAN said: 'In our daily life we should remember three things: joining the palms as in prayer, bowing as in worship, and charity. Joining the palms is the best posture for bringing the body and mind into a state of unity; the bow means honour and respect for others; charity is the basis of peace in society. If we practise them, it is certain that we shall in turn receive. Again there is a phrase most important for daily life: "For the ideal, seek the high; for the practice, honour the low." It is an old Zen saying: "His will treads the head of Vairochana; his practice is to prostrate himself at the feet of a child." It should be pondered deeply. The ideal must be as high and noble as possible, namely a consciousness which would set its shoe on the head of the truth-body of Vairochana Buddha. But the practice must honour the lowly. In humility he puts himself among the meanest.'

MASTER HAKUIN said: 'Suppose that, among the dense crowds of people in the hurly-burly of the market place, a man accidentally loses two or three pieces of gold. You will never find anyone who, because the place is noisy and bustling or because he has dropped his pieces of gold in the dirt, will not turn back to look for them. He pushes any number of people about, stirs up a lot of dust, and, weeping copious tears, rushes around searching for his gold. If he doesn't get it back into his own two hands, he will never regain his peace of mind. Do you consider the priceless jewel worn in the hair, your own inherent marvellous Tao, of less value than two or three pieces of gold!'

★ LIII ★

HERE IS a poem by Master Chosha:

Those who study the Way
Do not know the real,
Because from the first they recognize
Only the perceiving mind.
That which from the beginningless beginning
Has been the source of birth and death,
This it is that stupid men
Call the original body.

★ LIV ★

MASTER SEKITO said: 'The Three Worlds [of desire, form, and the formless one] and the Six Ways [or States, page 4] are only appearances arising in your own mind, like reflections of the moon in water, or images seen in a mirror.'

* LV *

MASTER CHOKEI was asked: 'What is meant by the True Dharma Eye?' 'Just don't sling dirt about,' was the Master's curt reply.

* LVI *

MASTER UMMON said: 'Though he speaks of fire, his mouth does not get burnt.'

* LVII *

MASTER KYOGEN stated: 'The painted picture of a dumpling does not take one's hunger away.'

* LVIII *

IN FEUDAL Japan a renowned Confucian scholar visited a Zen Master. 'As you may be aware, I have studied the Confucian learning, and I have a good understanding of what the Way is. But as the way of Zen seems to be somewhat different, I have come to ask whether you would be so good as to tell me something of it.' The Master unexpectedly slapped him smack on his face. In his surprise and confusion, the scholar found himself outside the room, and the Master quietly got up, pulled the door to, and went back to his seat. The samurai scholar was furious to think of how he had instinctively fled, and in the corridor stood fingering his sword-hilt, glaring at the door. A young monk, seeing his threatening posture, inquired what was the matter. 'Why', was the reply, 'nothing at all. Merely an insult from your Master. Service under three generations of my feudal lord, and never anyone

59

dared to lay a finger .. and now this Master! But he can't treat the honour of a samurai like that! I'll finish him off! . . .' The scowling countenance told that he meant it. The young monk said he did not understand it at all but doubtless it would be made clear later, so would not the guest have tea first? He led the way to the tea-room, where he poured out a cup for him. The scholar had the tea to his lips and was about to drink when the monk unexpectedly tapped the arm holding the cup. The tea spilled over everything. The monk confronted the Confucian and said: 'You claimed to have a good understanding of the Way. Now what is the Way?' The scholar tried to find some phrase from the Four Books or the Five Classics but failed and hesitated. The other raised his voice: 'What is the Way? Quick, speak, speak!' But he could think of nothing. The monk said: 'We have been very rude, but will you be introduced to our Way?' The Confucian had never come with the intention of being instructed by some young monk like this, but as his own way had failed him he perforce agreed. Then the Zen monk picked up a cloth and mopped up the spilt tea, saying: 'This is our Way,' and the Confucian, without thinking, said: 'Yes.' He had a flash of realization and saw that though he had known in theory that the Way was near at hand and could never be left for a moment, still he had been seeking it afar. He changed his whole thinking and returned to the Master's room for instruction. After years of intense practice he became a well-known figure in the spiritual history of that time.

A YOUNG man who had a bitter disappointment in life went to a remote monastery and said to the Master: 'I am disillusioned with life and wish to attain enlightenment to be freed from these sufferings. But I have no capacity for sticking long at anything. I could never do long years of meditation and study and austerity; I should relapse and be drawn back to the world again, painful though I know it to be. Is there any short way for people like me?' 'There is,' said the Master, 'if you are really determined. Tell me, what have you studied, what have you concentrated on most in your life?' 'Why, nothing really. We were rich, and I did not have to work. I suppose the thing I was really interested in was chess. I spent most of my time at that.'

The Master thought for a moment, and then said to his attendant: 'Call such and such a monk, and tell him to bring a chessboard and men.' The monk came with the board and the Master set up the pieces. He sent for a sword and showed it to the two. 'O monk,' he said, 'you have vowed obedience to me as your Master, and now I require it of you. You will play a game of chess with this youth, and if you lose I shall cut off your head with this sword. But I promise that you will be reborn in the Pure Land. If you win, I shall cut off the head of this man; chess is the only thing he has ever tried hard at, and if he loses he deserves to lose his head also.' They looked at the Master's face and saw that he meant it: he would cut off the head of the loser. Then they began to play. With the opening moves the youth felt the sweat trickling down to his heels as he played for his life. The chessboard became the whole world; he was entirely concentrated on it. At first he had somewhat the worst of it, but then the other made an inferior move and he seized his chance to launch a strong attack. As his opponent's position crumbled, he looked covertly at him. He saw a face of intelligence and sincerity, worn with years of austerity and effort. He thought of his own worthless life, and a wave of compassion came over him. He deliberately made a blunder and then another blunder, ruining his position and leaving himself defenceless. The Master suddenly leant forward and upset the board. The two contestants sat stupefied. 'There is no winner and no loser,' said the Master slowly, 'there is no head to fall here. Only two things are required,' and he turned to the young man, 'complete concentration, and compassion. You have today learnt them both. You were completely concentrated on the game, but then in that concentration you could feel compassion and sacrifice your life for it. Now stay here a few months and pursue our training in this spirit and your awakening is sure.'

* LX *

THE GREAT dragon on the ceiling of the main hall of the Myoshin-ji temple was painted by the famous Kano Tanyu. At that time the Master of Myoshin-ji was Master Gudo, renowned as the teacher of the emperor. He had heard that the dragons painted by

Tanyu were so realistic that when a ceiling on which one had been painted fell down by chance, some said it had been caused by the movement of the dragon's tail. When the painting of the dragon at Myoshin-ji was mooted, Gudo went to the painter's house and told him: 'For this special occasion I particularly want to have the painting of the dragon done from life.' Naturally the painter was taken aback, and he said: 'This is most unexpected. As a matter of fact, I am ashamed to say that I have never seen a living dragon.' He would have refused the commission. The Zen Master, however, agreed that it would be unreasonable to expect a painting of a living dragon from an artist who had never seen one, but told him to try to have a look at one as soon as he could. The painter asked wonderingly: 'Where can one see a living dragon? Where do they dwell?' 'Oh, that's nothing. At my place there are any number. Come and see them and paint one.' Tanyu joyfully went with the Master and when they arrived, at once asked: 'Well, here I am to see the dragons. Where are they?' The Master, letting his gaze go round the room, replied: 'Plenty of them here; can't you see them? What a pity!' The painter felt overcome with regret, and in the event spent the next two years with Master Gudo, practising Zen assiduously. One day something happened, and he rushed excitedly to the Master, saying: 'By your grace I have today seen the form of a live dragon!' 'Oh, have you? Good. But tell me, what did his roar sound like?' At this query the painter was again at a loss, and for one further year laboured on at his spiritual practices.

What he painted at the end of the year was the dragon of Myoshin-ji, a supreme masterpiece in the history of art, remarkable for its technique but far more for the life which the artist has infused into it. It seems as if it contains the great Life which embraces heaven and earth, the universe and man also. It was to pierce through to this reality that the master painter Tanyu poured out his heart's blood for three years. But when the one experience of reality was attained, there was no need to seek any further.

★ LXI ★

MASTER SESSAN said: 'It is not by chance that in the Buddhist code the virtue of rejoicing at the welfare of others surpasses even giving. Truly a noble thing, sublime and meritorious, the virtue of rejoicing for others. Now up jumps someone enthusiastically: "I agree, rejoicing for others is a fine thing. What you have said is right, and from now on I shall go in for it. Instead of striving for merit by giving money or breaking my bones helping those public movements or charitable activities which are such a nuisance, I shall watch the others doing it and afterwards rejoice and tell them how well they have done and how praiseworthy it all is! How fortunate that rejoicing rates higher than giving! What a wonderful religion Buddhism is!" This is the greatest of errors. He who can rejoice from his heart at the good deeds of another could never be satisfied unless he himself were performing them also. There is praise and rejoicing in hearing the Dharma, but the real virtue is to feel them from the heart at all right actions. And the error is not just a question of not doing right actions oneself, but being envious of them in others and wanting to spoil them, ending up as a mere tool of the passions arising from narrow selfishness, a mere slave to name and profit.'

★ LXII ★

MASTER SESSAN said: 'The illustrious Emperor Kiso of the T'ang Dynasty in China once made a visit to the Kinzanji temple on the Yangtze river. At the temple the scenery is exceptionally fine, and the throne was set at the top of the temple tower, giving the best view of the river. The emperor was conducted to his seat. He saw on the great river countless boats, some going up and some going down, some to the right and some to the left, so that it might almost have been mistaken for the sea. He was overjoyed to see the prosperity of the country he ruled: trade and commerce thus flourishing. At his side was standing Zen Master Obaku, and the emperor remarked to him: "How many flying sails on the river, I wonder?" The Master smoothed his robe and replied respectfully: "Only two." The emperor's satisfied expression was wiped off his face. What did he mean, with his two ships? Even now in front of one's very eyes were there not at least a hundred, perhaps two hundred? Two ships indeed! Was he making light of his emperor, laughing at him and making a fool of him? His face showed that the reply was not pardoned. "How two ships?" he asked. Master Obaku's expression showed not the slightest disturbance. Respectfully he answered: "Here are only the ship of name and the ship of profit." Name means seeking for reputation, and profit means seeking for gain. "As Your Majesty sees, there are many ships on the river, but one half of them are sailing for fame, and the other half to make money. The ship of name and the ship of profit—only these two are on the river." Pondering a thought, the emperor gave a deep sigh; it was as the abbot had said. He gave sweeping orders for reform which resulted in the famous T'ang culture.'

★ LXIII ★

BEFORE the Meiji Restoration (1868) Zen Master Kendo, a great spiritual figure, was Master of the Yoken-ji temple of Saheki, in Kyushu. This was the temple of the Mori clan, and one of their chief retainers had taken to unbridled extravagance and luxury and was sunk in a life of dissoluteness. The Master, thinking it a pity, remonstrated with him a few times, but instead of listening he resented the interference, and began to search for some pretext to have the Master disgraced. The Master, however, was one of very holy life, inwardly and outwardly pure, without a single opening for criticism. But a rumour arose that every night the Master, when the rest had gone to sleep, used to have a sumptuous repast in the privacy of his room. The retainer seized on this, and when all was dark crept into the temple garden and up to the Master's room. He confirmed that the Master was eating with apparent relish. Full of joy at having caught

66

his enemy, he presented himself the next morning at the court of the feudal lord. The head of the Mori clan was Lord Takayasu, a man of intelligence and furthermore a devout follower of the Master, but when he heard the story he was taken aback, and thinking it must be true, concealed himself in the garden the next night. When he peeped into the Master's room, sure enough the Master was eating away. Without more ado Lord Takayasu burst through the window into the room. The surprised Master quickly covered the bowl from which he was eating and put it out of sight, then inquired: 'To what urgent affair do we owe the honour of a visit at this unusual hour? Please pardon the absence of ceremony in receiving Your Grace.' The Lord replied sternly: 'There is no room for pardoning here. What have you just hidden away?' The Master earnestly asked that the matter be overlooked, repeatedly excusing himself and bowing to the ground. The nobleman refused to listen and made to seize the bowl by force, upon which the Master reluctantly showed him its contents. He said: 'I am ashamed that this should have come to the notice of Your Grace. There are many student monks who come here from different parts of the country, and though I am always impressing on them not to waste even a drop of water or throw away lightly a scrap of vegetable or grain of rice, there are so many of them, and most of them young, that in spite of all I say the cut-off ends of vegetables and rice leavings still get thrown away down the kitchen wastepipe. To stop this waste I fixed a small sieve at the end, and when they are all asleep I collect what is in it, boil it, and have it for my own evening meal. I have been doing this now for many years. I very much regret that such a sordid story should trouble your august ears.'

Hearing this, the lord was profoundly moved, and with tears in his eyes begged that his own conduct be excused.

⋆ LXIV ⋆

MASTER BASO asked Master Hyakujo what truth he taught. Master Hyakujo raised his fly-whisk. Baso said: 'Is that all? Nothing else?' Master Hyakujo lowered his fly-whisk.

⋆ LXV ⋆

TWO MONKS were going along, talking together. One said, 'If within life and death there were no Buddha, there would be no life and death.' The other said, 'If the Buddha were within life and death, there would be no delusion with regard to life and death.' They argued back and forth, and there was no end to it. Finally they climbed up to the monastery and asked Master Daibai about it. One asked: 'Of these two opinions, which is the more intimate?' Master Daibai said: 'One is more intimate, one is more distant.' 'Which is the intimate one?' asked the monk. 'Go away and ask me again tomorrow,' said Master Daibai. The next day the monk came again and asked. Master Daibai said, 'An intimate one does not ask. One who asks is not intimate.' The monk afterwards said: 'At the time I was with Master Daibai, I lost my Buddha-eye.'

⋆ LXVI ⋆

WHEN MASTER DAIBAI was about to die, he said to his monks: 'What comes is not to be avoided, what goes is not to be followed.' A little afterwards he heard a flying-squirrel screech and said: 'This is just this, and nothing else. You all keep this faithfully. Now I must depart.'

⋆ LXVII ⋆

MASTER SOKEI-AN says of this moment: 'When this comes you can do nothing more. Close your eyes and join your hands. Go with that which is not yours back to that original state whence you have come!'

⋆ LXVIII ⋆

MASTER NANSEN, asked by a monk, 'Where does he go who knows what is what?' replied: 'He becomes an ox of the monastery supporter down the hill, to requite him for his help.' When the monk thanked him for his teaching, the Master added: 'At midnight yesterday, the moon shone in at the window.'

⋆ LXIX ⋆

ASKED at another time, 'Where will the Master be gone to in a hundred years' time?' Master Nansen replied: 'I'll be a water-buffalo.' The monk asked: 'May I follow you or not?' Master Nansen said: 'If you do, bring a mouthful of grass with you!'

MASTER SHIKO said in a poem:

Thirty years I have lived on Shiko Mountain;
Twice daily a meal of gruel was enough to keep fit.
I climb up the mountain and come back safely.
People who come to me, do they know me, or not?

★ L X X I ★

A MONK asked Master Roso: 'What is the wordless word?' Master Roso said: 'Where is your mouth?' The monk said: 'I do not have one.' 'What do you eat with then?' asked the Master. The monk had no reply.

★ L X X I I ★

MASTER NANSEN was washing clothes. A monk asked: 'Is the Master still doing such things?' Master Nansen, holding up his clothes, asked: 'What is to be done with them?'

★ L X X I I I ★

A MONK asked Master Joshu: 'What is the Buddha?' 'The one in the Hall.' The monk said: 'The one in the Hall is an image, a lump of mud.' Joshu agreed: 'That is so.' 'What is the Buddha?' persisted the monk. 'The one in the Hall.'

★ L X X I V ★

MASTER JOSHU was a disciple and heir of Master Nansen. When Joshu first came to him, Master

Nansen lived in the Hermitage of the Auspicious Image. The Master was resting in his room. Seeing a new monk come in, he asked: 'Where have you just come from?' Joshu said: 'From the Hermitage of the Auspicious Image.' 'Do you see the Auspicious Image?' asked Master Nansen. 'I do not,' said Joshu, 'but I see a Tathagata ['thus come', appellation of Buddha] lying down.' Master Nansen sat up and asked: 'Are you a monk with a master, or master-less?' 'I am a monk with a master,' replied Joshu. 'Who is this master of yours?' queried Nansen. Joshu said: 'It is early spring and still cold; I am profoundly grateful to find my respected and blessed Master in good health.' Master Nansen called his attendant and said to him: 'Put this monk up somewhere.'

* LXXV *

A MONK who had been with Master Kassan went on pilgrimage around all the Zen places, but found nothing to suit him anywhere. Moreover, everywhere he heard Master Kassan praised as a very great master. So he returned, and asked Master Kassan: 'You are known to have a profound understanding; why did you not reveal it to me?' Master Kassan replied: 'When you boiled rice, did I not light the fire? When you handed out food, did I not hold out my bowl to receive it? When did I betray your expectations?' At this, the monk awakened.

* LXXVI *

A NUN asked Master Joshu: 'What is the mysterious secret?' The Master tapped her on the elbow. She

71

said: 'You are still holding on to something.' 'No,'
said Master Joshu, 'it is you who are holding on to it!'

MASTER GENSHA once said to his monks: 'Everywhere
there is great concern about the means to bring about
the liberation of sentient beings. [This is the first of
the Four Vows.] But if you come across a blind deaf
mute, what then? He could not see your gestures, nor
hear your preaching, and he could not even ask a
question. Yet if you fail to help him, you are worthless.'

ONE OF his monks went to ask Master Ummon about
this. 'Make your obeisance,' ordered Master Ummon.
As he stood up from it, Master Ummon made as if to
strike him. The monk jerked back. 'So you are not
blind,' said Master Ummon, 'come near.' The monk
did as bidden. 'And you are not deaf, either. Do you
understand?' 'Understand what?' asked the monk
perplexed. 'Nor are you dumb,' commented Master
Ummon. On hearing these words the monk awoke
as from a deep sleep.

A MONK came to see Master Gasan. Before he had even
made his obeisance, the Master held out his hand
asking: 'Why is this called a hand?' Then, before the
monk could reply, stretched out a leg, asking: 'And
why is this called a leg?' The monk opened his mouth
and was about to reply when Master Gasan clapped his

hands together and laughed. The startled monk withdrew without a word. Next day he came again, and Master Gasan cautioned him: 'These days Zen practitioners are given to trifling with the precious problems. Without properly disciplining themselves, they are very quick to make comments or write poems on the problems. They are no better than windbags, and not one of them would make a good teacher. If you really want Zen, give up as worthless everything you have learned and experienced. Apply yourself single-mindedly. Die and then be reborn!' At this, the monk suddenly awakened.

* LXXX *

A MONK came to see Master Hogen, who asked him where he came from. He replied: 'From Master Joshu.' Master Hogen said: 'Does not Joshu teach "the oak tree in the garden"?' The monk denied it. Master Hogen insisted: 'But everyone says that when asked about the "meaning of Bodhidharma's coming from the West", Joshu answered, "The oak tree in the front garden". How can you deny it?' The monk said: 'My master said nothing of the kind. Please do not insult the late Master.' Master Hogen commented: 'Truly, you are a lion's cub!'

* LXXXI *

MASTER KYOGEN said: 'My poverty last year was not real poverty, but this year my poverty is real. Though last year there was no place even for an awl to stick into, this year I have no awl either.'

MASTER KANKEI had trained under Master Rinzai, and completed his training under Master Massan (the nun 'End-Mountain').

When he first came to Master Rinzai and entered his room for an interview, Master Rinzai grabbed him by his collar. Kankei said: 'I see, I see!' The Master let go of him and said: 'I pardon you twenty blows!' Kankei stayed and trained under him. Later he used to say: 'When I saw Master Rinzai, there was no talking or explanation. Now I am no longer hungry.' From there he went to Master Massan, deciding: 'If what she says hits the mark I will remain there. If not, I will overturn her Zen Seat [the high chair from which Zen Masters taught or gave interviews].' He entered the Hall, and she sent someone to ask: 'Have you come on a trip to see the mountains, or have you come for the sake of Buddhism?' When he said for the latter, she ascended her Seat. He came up to it. Master Massan said: 'Where did you come from today?' He replied: 'From Roko.' 'Why don't you put down your bundle of luggage?' asked the Master. Kankei had no reply and bowed, asking: 'What is Massan (End-Mountain)?' She answered: 'It does not show its peak.' He asked: 'Who is Massan's master?' She answered: 'There is no real form of men and women.' Kankei gave a Katsu (Rinzai's 'style') and asked again: 'Why then do you not change and disappear?' Master Massan said: 'I am not a god; I am not a demon; what could I change?' Kankei knelt down and stayed, working in the garden.

Later, having settled down, Master Kankei said from the High Seat: 'When I was with Uncle Rinzai I got half a ladle of rice, and when I was with Aunt Massan, I received half a ladle of gruel. Together they made one ladle, and I ate it up. Now I am full and snoring.'

* LXXXIII *

MASTER TENNO was asked by a monk: 'I have been with you for three years, and received no teaching from you. Why?' The Master said: 'Have I not been teaching you ever since you arrived?' 'When did you give me any teaching!' asked the monk. Master Tenno said: 'When you brought me tea, I received it from you. When you bowed to me, I inclined my head to you. When did I not teach you?' While the monk was still pondering this, Master Tenno added: 'When you look, just look. If you wonder about it, you won't get to the point.' On this, the monk awakened.

* LXXXIV *

A MONK on pilgrimage had visited great Masters without being able to settle what he felt still lacking. Rather dejected he came to Master Tokusan and asked him: 'Is it possible for me, too, to share the Supreme Teachings with the patriarchs?' Master Tokusan hit him and said: 'What are you talking about?' Next day he asked for an explanation. Master Tokusan said: 'My teaching has no words and sentences. It has nothing to give anybody.' At this, the monk awakened.

A MONK said to Master Seppo: 'I have shaved my head, taken the robe, received the vows—why am I not considered to be a Buddha?' Master Seppo said: 'There is nothing better than an absence of goodness.'

* LXXXVI *

A MONK asked Master Gensha: 'The old masters, when they raised the stick or lifted up the fly-whisk—did they thus bring out the essence of Zen?' 'They did not,' said the Master. The monk asked: 'What was the meaning of their actions?' Master Gensha raised his fly-whisk. The monk asked: 'What is the essence of Buddhism?' The Master said: 'When you have awakened you will know.'

* LXXXVII *

MASTER GENSHA was eating cakes with a general who asked: 'What is that which we use every day, but do not know it?' The Master offered him a cake, 'Do have one.' The general ate it and repeated his question. Master Gensha said: 'We use it every day, but we do not know it.'

* LXXXVIII *

SEEING a monk approach, Master Rakan raised his fly-whisk. The monk made obeisance. Master Rakan said: 'Why did you bow?' 'Out of gratitude,' said the monk. The Master struck him and said: 'You tell me you bowed when you saw me raise my fly-whisk; why

do you not thank me every day when you see me sweep
the ground or clean the floor?'

* LXXXIX *

MASTER RINZAI came to the tomb of Bodhidharma.
The incumbent asked: 'Will your first bow be to the
Buddha or to the Patriarch?' Master Rinzai answered:
'Neither to the one nor to the other.' The incumbent
asked: 'What quarrel is there between you and the
Buddha and Patriarch?' Master Rinzai left.

* XC *

MASTER TANKA, staying in a temple in mid-winter,
used one of the wooden images to make a fire.
(To destroy images is one of the Five Heinous
Crimes.) The incumbent came running: 'What are
you doing?' 'Burning a wooden statue.' 'But it's a
Buddha!' Stirring up the ashes, Master Tanka asked:
'Can you see any sharira?' (reliquary stones said to
remain in the ashes of saints). 'How can you expect to
find sharira in a wooden statue?' 'Oh well, if it is
only that,' said Master Tanka, 'may I have another
one to keep warm?'

* XCI *

ON A COLD winter day a masterless samurai came to
Master Eisai and begged him: 'I am poor and sick; my
family is dying of hunger. Please, Master, help us.'
Master Eisai, being used to austerities and equally poor,
had nothing to give him. Then he remembered the
Buddha image in the Hall. He went, took off its halo,

and gave it to the samurai: 'Sell this, it should tide you over.' Though bewildered, the samurai was desperate, so he took it and left. One of the monks was horror-struck. 'What have you done, Master? This is sacrilege!' 'Sacrilege, my word! Haven't you heard of Master Tanka who burned a Buddha image to warm himself? Surely what I have done is not half as bad. I have merely put the Buddha's heart, which is full of love and mercy, to use. Had he himself heard that poor samurai's plight, he'd have cut off one of his limbs for him!'

⋆ XCII ⋆

A MONK asked of Master Sosan: 'Please sprinkle the compassion of your teaching so that I may be liberated.' 'Who has put you under restraint?' asked the Master. 'No one.' Master Sosan said: 'Why then do you ask to be liberated?' At this, the monk awakened fully.

⋆ XCIII ⋆

MASTER YOKA cautions: 'Getting rid of things and clinging to emptiness are the same illness. It is like throwing oneself into fire to avoid being drowned.'

⋆ XCIV ⋆

MASTER DOGEN said: 'The flower petals fall though we love them, the weeds grow through we hate them— that is just how it is.'

⋆ XCV ⋆

MASTER DOSHIN said: 'The wise man does nothing; the fool ties himself up.'

★ XCVI ★

MASTER RINZAI said: 'When hungry, I eat; when tired, I sleep. Fools laugh at me. The wise understand.'

★ XCVII ★

MASTER SOZAN said: 'Hide your good deeds and keep your functioning secret. Look like a simpleton or fool.'

★ XCVIII ★

AN old poem points out:

Faults and delusions
Are not to be got rid of
Just blindly.
Look at the astringent persimmons!
They turn into the sweet dried ones.

★ XCIX ★

MASTER SOKEI-AN tells us that 'Zen makes a religion of tranquillity.' He says: 'These days human beings have forgotten what religion is. They have forgotten a peculiar love which unites their human nature to Great Nature. This love has nothing to do with human love. Standing in the midst of nature you feel this love of Great Nature. . . . Zen students must experience this peculiar love. This is religion.'

★ C ★

AN OLD gentleman came to ask Master Taian for help. He had been chamberlain at court, but was now retired. His children were grown up and married. Recently his wife had died, and he was desperately lonely. He felt he could no longer cope, and had come to see the Master as his last hope. Master Taian pondered what could be done. To suggest formal sitting meditation was unlikely to help. Sitting in the stiff formal position through audiences as the old gentleman had done most of his life, why, he had done enough of this. Should he put him to contemplate nature? Yet, however healing that might be, would he, cultured old gentleman that he was, be able to? Thoroughly at home in the vast poetry collection, would not an appropriate verse rise up in his mind and prevent him from the immediacy of seeing? What could be done for him? Then Master Taian suggested: 'Go back home. And the next time you feel really desperate, then go into your innermost room, shut the door so that you are all alone and unobserved, and there, without deliberation or thinking of to whom, what for, or why, do nine full prostrations. Just when you really feel desperate, you can lay yourself down simply, with the trust of a little child, for no reason, and expecting nothing. And see what happens.' Tears were in the old gentleman's eyes as he thanked him and departed. A couple of months later he came again. 'My life has changed. Will you take me as your disciple?' 'You look happy these days,' said Master Taian, 'is there anything else?' 'No,' replied he, 'thanks to your help, all is well.' 'Then why not apply it?' asked Master Taian.

New Directions Paperbooks—a partial listing

César Aira, Ghosts
Paul Auster, The Red Notebook
Djuna Barnes, Nightwood
Charles Baudelaire, The Flowers of Evil
Bei Dao, The August Sleepwalker
Roberto Bolaño, By Night in Chile
    Last Evenings on Earth
Jorge Luis Borges, Labyrinths
Kamau Brathwaite, Middle Passages
Basil Bunting, Complete Poems
Anne Carson, Glass, Irony & God
Horacio Castellanos Moya, Senselessness
José Camilo Cela,
    Mazurka for Two Dead Men
Louis-Ferdinand Céline,
    Journey to the End of the Night
Inger Christensen, alphabet
Julio Cortázar, Cronopios & Famas
Robert Creeley, If I Were Writing This
Osamu Dazai, The Setting Sun
H. D., Trilogy
Robert Duncan, Selected Poems
Eça de Queirós, The Maias
Shusaku Endo, Deep River
Jenny Erpenbeck, The Book of Words
Lawrence Ferlinghetti,
    A Coney Island of the Mind
    Poetry as Insurgent Art
F. Scott Fitzgerald, The Crack-Up
Forrest Gander, As a Friend
Hermann Hesse, Siddhartha
Takashi Hiraide,
    For the Fighting Spirit of the Walnut (bilingual)
Susan Howe, My Emily Dickinson
Bohumil Hrabal, I Served the King of England
Christopher Isherwood, Berlin Stories
B. S. Johnson, The Unfortunates
Franz Kafka, Amerika: The Man Who Disappeared
Denise Levertov, Selected Poems
Clarice Lispector, The Hour of the Star
Federico García Lorca, Selected Poems
Nathaniel Mackey, Splay Anthem
Javier Marías, Your Face Tomorrow (3 volumes)
Thomas Merton, New Seeds of Contemplation
Henry Miller, The Air-Conditioned Nightmare
    Big Sur & The Oranges of Hieronymus Bosch

Yukio Mishima, Confessions of a Mask
Vladimir Nabokov, Laughter in the Dark
Pablo Neruda, Love Poems (bilingual)
    Residence on Earth (bilingual)
George Oppen, New Collected Poems (with CD)
Wilfred Owen, Collected Poems
Michael Palmer, The Company of Moths
Nicanor Parra, Antipoems
Kenneth Patchen, The Walking-Away World
Octavio Paz,
    The Collected Poems 1957–1987 (bilingual)
Ezra Pound, Cantos
    Selected Poems of Ezra Pound
Raymond Queneau, Exercises in Style
Kenneth Rexroth,
    Written on the Sky: Poems from the Japanese
Rainer Maria Rilke, The Possibility of Being
Arthur Rimbaud,
    A Season in Hell and The Drunken Boat
Guillermo Rosales, The Halfway House
Jean-Paul Sartre, Nausea
Delmore Schwartz,
    In Dreams Begin Responsibilities
W. G. Sebald, The Emigrants
    The Rings of Saturn
C. H. Sisson, Selected Poems
Stevie Smith, New Selected Poems
Gary Snyder, Turtle Island
Muriel Spark, Memento Mori
George Steiner, My Unwritten Books
Yoko Tawada, The Naked Eye
Dylan Thomas, Selected Poems 1934–1952
Uwe Timm, The Invention of Curried Sausage
Tomas Tranströmer,
    The Great Enigma: New Collected Poems
Leonid Tsypkin, Summer in Baden-Baden
Enrique Vila-Matas, Bartleby & Co.
Robert Walser, The Assistant
Eliot Weinberger, An Elemental Thing
Nathanael West,
    Miss Lonelyhearts & The Day of the Locust
Tennessee Williams, The Glass Menagerie
    A Streetcar Named Desire
William Carlos Williams, Selected Poems
    In the American Grain
    Paterson

For a complete listing, request a free catalog from New Directions, 80 8th Avenue, NY NY 10011
or visit us online at www.ndpublishing.com.